Resolving the Paradox of Jean-Jacques Rousseau's Sexual Politics

Tamela Ice

University Press of America,® Inc.
Lanham • Boulder • New York • Toronto • Plymouth, UK

Copyright © 2009 by
University Press of America,® Inc.
4501 Forbes Boulevard
Suite 200
Lanham, Maryland 20706
UPA Acquisitions Department (301) 459-3366

Estover Road
Plymouth Pl6 7PY
United Kingdom

All rights reserved
Printed in the United States of America
British Library Cataloging in Publication Information Available

Library of Congress Control Number: 2009923219
ISBN: 978-0-7618-4477-8 (paperback : alk. paper)

∞ ™ The paper used in this publication meets the minimum
requirements of American National Standard for Information
Sciences—Permanence of Paper for Printed Library Materials,
ANSI Z39.48—1984

This book is dedicated to D.

Je vous penserai à souvent avec l'affection

Contents

A Note on Translations		vii
Preface		ix
Acknowledgments		xiii
I	Rousseau's Philosophy of Servitude: 'Woman' Defined	1
	Introduction	1
	Rousseau's Identity Politics	3
	Rousseau's Sexual Politics	11
	Woman's Duties	17
	The Education of 'Woman'	19
	Concluding Remarks	22
II	The Other Side of the Paradox	28
	Introduction	28
	Contemporary Interpretations	28
	Rousseau's Philosophical Orientation	30
	Rousseau's Philosophical Project and Works	31
	Concluding Remarks	38
III	Rousseau and the Nineteenth Century Novel of Female Adultery: Alienation, Psychological Oppression, and Bad Faith in Rousseau and Flaubert	41
	Introduction	41
	Psychological Oppression	43
	Bad Faith	45
	The Novel of Female Adultery	47

	Rousseau's Adulterous Woman: Sophie	49
	Flaubert's Madame Bovary and Emma	52
	Concluding Remarks	58
IV	Rousseau and Simone de Beauvoir: Overcoming Alienation, Psychological Oppression, and Bad Faith through Liberty	61
	Introduction	61
	Rousseau and Contemporary Feminism	62
	Beauvoir's Rejection of Essentialism and Women's Responsibility	65
	Liberty in Beauvoir and Rousseau	66
	Beauvoir's Woman of Bad Faith: Monique	69
Conclusion		77
Bibliography		85

A Note On Translations

The translations of Rousseau, Flaubert, and Beauvoir are my own, with the assistance of Dr. John T. Booker, in the French Department at the University of Kansas. I have preserved the spelling and grammatical errors as they appear in the French versions of the texts. Moreover, I have attempted to preserve as literal a translation as possible. Any errors in translation are my own.

Preface

Jean-Jacques Rousseau is one of the most important thinkers on the topics of social freedom and inequality, and his views of these matters are typically taken to be progressive. Rousseau laments the ways in which modern society and governments deprive persons of their natural freedom and enslave them through their false desires and passions. He takes citizens to be equal members of the social contract, and his philosophy attempts to show how men can be raised and governed to appreciate and protect their own freedom and that of their fellow men. However, Rousseau's views on women sits in tension with his philosophy of freedom and equality. On the one hand, Rousseau argues that women are naturally equal to men. On the other hand, he sees women not as potential citizens but as the servants of men. This presents the interpreter of Rousseau with something of a paradox: Rousseau is the philosopher of freedom for men and yet the philosopher of servitude for women. This paradox is referred to in the literature as "the paradox of Jean-Jacques Rousseau's sexual politics." Throughout this work, 'sexual politics' will be understood as the power-relations between the sexes. 'Power' in relations between people, for Rousseau, refers to the way in which one individual influences the beliefs, actions, and attitudes of another. Insofar as Rousseau locates woman's proper place within the home (as wife and mother), his sexual politics concerns the relationship between men and women in marriage.

Feminist philosophers have reacted to this paradox in a variety of ways. One attempt to resolve this paradox, and seek a "feminist-friendly" reading of Rousseau, is that of Nicole Fermon (*Domesticating Passions: Rousseau, Women, and Nation*) and Joel Schwartz (*The Sexual Politics of Jean-Jacques Rousseau*). Fermon and Schwartz reject only what Rousseau says about women in society, preserving the claim that women are equal to men, and jettisoning the view that women should be taught to be men's slaves.

This approach results in embracing the philosopher of freedom, and excusing the sexist.

Another reaction to the paradox presented in Rousseau is to reject the interpretation of Rousseau as a philosopher of freedom and to show that his entire philosophy is geared toward a hierarchical, communitarian political theory. This approach is taken by Penny A. Weiss (*A Gendered Community: Rousseau, Sex, and Politics*).

Carole Pateman (*The Disorder of Women: Democracy, Feminism and Political Thought* and *The Sexual Contract*) rejects both of the aforementioned reactions to the paradox in Rousseau. Pateman claims that, with regard to Rousseau's philosophical project, his philosophy of freedom for men and his philosophy of servitude for women are mutually reinforcing and dependent upon one another. According to Pateman, the paradox cannot be resolved, and in rejecting Rousseau's philosophy of servitude for women, one must also reject his philosophy of freedom for men. The freedom of men depends on the servitude of women.

As I see it, the reactions of Fermon, Schwartz, and Weiss are untenable positions. On this point I agree with Pateman. However, I disagree with Pateman's claim that the paradox of Rousseau's sexual politics cannot be resolved because, as I will argue, there *is* no paradox here if we see Rousseau as interested *only* in the freedom and equality of men. I shall argue that women are, for Rousseau, the means to an end.

In Chapter I, I will clarify one side of the paradox of Jean-Jacques Rousseau's sexual politics. That is, I will explicate the exact details of what Rousseau proposes as the ideal power relationship between men and women in marriage. Rousseau's sexual politics is grounded on his identity politics, or his version of essentialism (his definition of 'woman' in society). Rousseau's proposed domestic education for women socializes females for the power-structured marital relationship wherein Rousseau offers a justification for the servitude of women. Rousseau's philosophy of servitude for women results in the sexual objectification of women by themselves, by men, and by the state.

One cause for the mistaken views of Rousseau's paradox centers around confusions with regard to Rousseau's definitive philosophical project. According to Fermon, Rousseau's objective is to establish an egalitarian society and restore the "maternal" image to the state. Schwartz maintains that Rousseau attempts to establish *some* degree of equality between the sexes. Fermon and Schwartz agree that Rousseau establishes the *possibility* of liberty for women. Weiss understands Rousseau to be a communitarian, and his ultimate project as the establishment of a community of equal and free citizens. Pateman understands Rousseau's ultimate project to be his ideal state as put forth in *Du contrat social*. In Chapter II, I will argue that Rousseau's definitive philosophical project is the restoration and maximization of *man's* liberty. Rousseau's ideal state is in accordance with the *natural* liberty of *man*, which, in the civil state, depends on a domestic order wherein man's role in the family is in accordance with the nature of *man*, and this will be the result of an education (socialization) that is in accordance with the nature of *man*. In addition to restoring and maximizing man's liberty, Rousseau wants to restore a sense of equality among men (and he means males), the family, and virtue–to man and to the state. Woman's place in Rousseau's philosophical project is with regard to the restoration of virtue and the family. Chapter I and Chapter II will show that the paradox of Rousseau's sexual politics is merely apparent.

The tendency in the literature on Rousseau is to focus on women in the state or women in relation to men (within marriage). In Chapter III, I will shift the focus in order to develop a more complete account of the consequences of Rousseau's sexual politics, and sexual politics in general, and Rousseau's philosophical project. Rousseau's identity politics, sexual politics, and proposed domestic education for women were not new in his time and persisted into the nineteenth century (and are still common today). Rousseau preserves the institutional and interpersonal oppression of women. In this Chapter, I will illuminate the psychological implications of Rousseau's identity politics, sexual politics, and proposed domestic education (socialization) for women, namely self-alienation, psychological oppression, and bad faith. I will examine these consequences for women in Rousseau's unfinished novel *Les Solitaires* and Gustave Flaubert's social commentary, *Madame Bovary*.

Rousseau does not stand in opposition to all forms of feminism. In Chapter IV, I will explain Rousseau's affinities with two contemporary forms of feminism, namely the essentialism of cultural feminism (a form of essentialism which defines women in terms reminiscent of Rousseau) and a poststructural alternative (which claims that we cannot define woman as 'human' without denying the oppression of women). My principle objectives in this Chapter will be to illuminate logical problems for essentialism (or identity politics) and, with the aid of Simone de Beauvoir, I will explain how self-alienation, psychological oppression, and bad faith can be overcome. Finally, in this Chapter, I will propose a philosophy of liberation for women that integrates Beauvoir's account of liberty in *Pour une morale de l'ambiguité* and Rousseau's various senses of liberty. That is, I will show how, contrary to Pateman's claim, we can reject Rousseau's philosophy of servitude for women, and his definitive philosophical project for men, but appropriate his philosophy of freedom and apply this to *all* humans.

Acknowledgments

I want to thank my students for their interest in this work. I want to thank my Philosophy professors at Missouri State University (formerly Southwest Missouri State University) for believing in me and feeding my mind. I thank all of my graduate professors at the University of Kansas. For their assistance and encouragement in getting to this point, I want to give special thanks to John T. Booker, Ann Cudd, Anthony Genova, Rex Martin, and James Woelfel. There are others – too many to name. I thank you all.

I am deeply grateful for the support and encouragement of my colleagues at Kansas City Kansas Community College for their warm welcome and enthusiastic support. Thank you.

To my parents, Gene and Francis Ice, my brother, Ronnie Ice, my sister-in-law, Denise Ice, my sisters, Tina Bradshaw and Barbara Ice, and Grandma, Ellen – thank you. I want to thank all of the women I have known in my life, all of the men (the good and the bad). Through you, I learned what being a woman means for me, and how to work toward being the woman I want to be.

I also want to thank the editors at University Press of America for their assistance in preparing this work for publication.

There are so many individuals to thank – far too many to mention. I hope you all know who you are, and the extent of my gratitude.

I wish to thank Gallimard Publishing for permission to reprint from Simone de Beauvoir's *Tout compte fait* and *La femme rompue*, © Éditions Gallimard.

Chapter I

Rousseau's Philosophy of Servitude: 'Woman' Defined

INTRODUCTION

Chapters I and II will provide an internal analysis of the paradox of Jean-Jacques Rousseau's theory of the power relations between men and women in the marital relationship (i.e., Rousseau's sexual politics). For Rousseau, power in relationships "consists in the capacity to produce effects . . . changes in the life, attitudes, and behaviour [sic] of the possessor of power and of those upon whom he [or she] exerts his [or her] power."[1] Briefly stated, this paradox concerns the apparent disparity between Rousseau's philosophy of servitude for women, his sexual politics, and his definitive philosophical project, his philosophy of freedom for men. The issue to be determined in these two chapters is whether Rousseau's sexual politics is consistent with (i.e., reinforces) or contradictory to (i.e., undermines) his philosophical project. Chapter I and Chapter II in conjunction will show that the paradox of Jean Jacques Rousseau's sexual politics is merely apparent. Moreover, it will be clear that Rousseau's views on women (in his sexual politics and his overall project) reinforce the institutional and interpersonal oppression of women.

In order to adequately analyze this apparent paradox, it will be useful to have a clear understanding of Rousseau's theoretical treatise on woman,– what 'woman' *is* and what she *must* be in the civil state, the details of Rousseau's sexual politics, and his proposed domestic education for women. Rousseau's proposed domestic education for women is his idea of the proper socialization of females in preparation for the power-structured arrangement between the sexes in the marital relationship (his sexual politics). The foundation for Rousseau's domestic education for women and his sexual politics is his identity politics–his definition of 'woman' in the civil state, in terms of her sex, her duties, her purpose, and her inclinations (action-guiding passions–sometimes referred to as dispositions).

In shifting the focus away from Rousseau's account of man and his proposed domestic education for males, it is important to note that many of the important terms Rousseau uses with regard to humans (male and female) in his anthropological work, *Discours sur l'origine et les fondements de l'inégalité parmi les hommes*, are not used in reference to women in Book V of *Émile*. For example, in its primitive sense, *amour de soi* means self-preservation, the preservation of one's body and one's life. This passion concerns the individual in relation to himself. In the civil state, with regard to men, Rousseau redefines this term to include the preservation of man's individual liberty. The faculties of *amour de soi* are attack and defense. With regard to women, Rousseau discusses the faculties of attack and defense, and the preservation of women's social status as well as the preservation of the family. However, Rousseau does not use the term *amour de soi* in reference to woman.

Another important term in relation to man in the civil state is *pitié*, or compassion. This passion, or inclination, in its primitive sense, refers to the distaste one has for the suffering of others *like oneself*. In the civil state, with regard to men, this term is related to the ways in which man finds his moral footing with *other men* in society. This is the social/political passion. It also refers to man's compassion for those less fortunate. For woman, assuming her place in the moral order and her proper relationship to *a* man is crucial, but again, this term, '*pitié*', is not used in reference to women. Moreover, cultivating compassion for others is *not* included in the domestic education for women. For Rousseau, in the civil state, woman and man are different kinds of beings, and *pitié* refers to man's relationship to his own kind.

Yet another important term Rousseau uses with regard to man/men is *amour propre*, which is related to his notion of dependence on the will, opinions, and judgments of others. Part of Rousseau's understanding of individual liberty is being *independent* of the will, opinions, and judgments of others, deriving one's self-esteem and sense of value from within rather than from others (i.e., psychological liberty/independence). Rousseau makes women dependent upon the opinions and judgments of men, and society. In Book V of *Émile*, the term '*amour propre*' is alluded to in reference to woman, and Rousseau does explicitly state that woman is subject to the opinions and judgments of men and others in society. With that in mind, let us turn to Rousseau's theoretical account of woman in the civil state, his identity politics.

ROUSSEAU'S IDENTITY POLITICS

For Rousseau, 'woman' in the civil state is a social construct, defined by convention and the dominant ideology of his day. That is, "On ne naît pas femme: on le devient" ("One is not born woman: one becomes it/that").² In Book IV of *Émile*, Rousseau says,

> Jusqu'à l'âge nubile les enfans des deux séxes n'ont rien d'apparent qui les distingue; même visage, même figure, même teint, même voix, tout est égal; les filles sont des enfans, les garçons des enfans; le même nom suffit à des *êtres si semblables* . . . et les femmes ne perdant point cette même conformité semblent à bien des égards ne jamais être autre chose.³
>
> Until the nubile age children of both sexes have nothing apparent which distinguishes them; the same face, the same figure, the same complexion, the same voice, everything is equal; girls are children, boys are children; the same name suffices for *beings so similar* . . . and women not losing this same conformity seem properly in many respects never to be anything else.

This notion that woman is in some ways still a child was a commonly held view in Rousseau's time. For Rousseau (and commonly agreed to in his time), the nubile age (the marriageable age) is the point at which puberty occurs. This is when physical differences between the sexes will be noticeable. This is also, according to Rousseau, the time in life when sexual desires surface. Rousseau maintains that the transition from childhood to puberty varies in individuals according to their temperaments, and among groups according to climate. Puberty occurs earlier in warmer climates and in cities, and among learned and civilized peoples as opposed to barbarians.⁴ Rousseau is also of the opinion that puberty, and the accompanying sexual urges, occurs in females earlier than in males. Rousseau claims that since there is such diversity with regard to the onset of puberty, if children are kept in ignorance (not exposed to sexually enticing sights or individuals, such as prostitutes and the sexually promiscuous members of the aristocracy), childhood can be extended until the age of twenty. That is, puberty can be prolonged. Rousseau does not mean that one can control the development of the body. He means that the sexual awareness and urges can be prolonged. As soon as sexual desire is evidenced, it is best that the young are married. Thus, remaining a child is not simply a matter of having a child's body; it is having a child's innocence of sexuality and sexual matters.

Of paramount importance for Rousseau is what takes place from birth to the nubile age (puberty). Females, like males, possess the faculty of *perfectibilité*–the faculty of becoming (or the ability to become) other than what one is. Rousseau's primary objective in Book V of *Émile* is to propose a way of socializing females of the aristocracy so that future generations of aristocratic women will be *virtuous* women rather than continuing to become women who abandon their duties as wives and mothers, women who exert too much influence over men, and women whose acts of adultery lead to the decline of the family. In other words, Rousseau is addressing what he considered to be the "problem women of his time," the women of the Parisian aristocracy. N. J. H. Dent explains that in Rousseau,

> Humans can learn how their environment works, and can adapt their behaviour [sic] to it for their advantage, as well as modifying that environment for further advantage. Virtually all human behaviours [sic] are learned or acquired, and few become so consolidated as not to allow modification if need (or taste [judgment]) requires it.[5]

This positive aspect of *perfectibilité* is the emphasis of Rousseau's proposed domestic educations for both males and females. The negative aspect is that this faculty can be used in ways that are *disadvantageous*, which is what Rousseau thinks happened in the movement from the original state to his present time. *Perfectibilité* can give rise to all the virtues *or* all the vices human beings are capable of.[6] Insofar as females possess this faculty of *perfectibilité*, the behaviors (and beliefs) of females (and males) can be manipulated, and females can *become* what Rousseau thinks they *must* become in the civil state. That is, females can become 'woman.'

Rousseau does not deny that females *could* be educated (both formally and domestically) in the same manner as males. The education of females, Rousseau asserts, is the business of mothers, and mothers are not prevented from educating their daughters in whatever manner they please. However, Rousseau issues a caution to mothers. If women are educated in the same manner as men, they will be more like men. It is only through their differences, Rousseau maintains, that women have any value or power. If women and men are more alike, then men really will be the masters of women (as opposed to *appearing* to be their masters).[7] Moreover, Rousseau adds, cultivating the qualities of man in women, and in the process neglecting the qualities that are proper to women, "c'est donc visiblement travailler à leur prejudice"[8] ("is then visibly working to their detriment"). According to Rousseau, women would be unable to reconcile and manage the co-existence of the qualities appropriate for man and those appropriate for woman—"parce qu'ils sont incompatibles"[9] ("because they are incompatible"). This is a familiar claim in our own time as women struggle to balance a career and the home life. Rousseau never adequately explains why these qualities are incompatible, nor does he consider cultivating the qualities he assigns to men and women equally. He merely makes the claim. He *does*, however, offer a utilitarian justification for *not* educating women in the same manner as men—". . . mère judicieuse . . . faites en une honnête-femme, et soyez sure qu'elle en vaudra mieux pour elle et pour nous"[10] ("judicious mother . . . make of her a decent woman, and be certain that she will be worth more [because of it] for herself and for us"). Again, Rousseau is not interested in what women *could* be, or what 'woman,' as a social construct, could be. His concern is with what he thinks the definition of 'woman', and women, *must* be.

Rousseau begins his theoretical treatise on woman with the claim that females, "doit être femme . . . c'est à dire, avoir tout ce qui convient à la constitution de son espece et de son sexe pour remplir sa place dans l'ordre physique et moral" ("must be woman . . . that is to say, having everything which is appropriate to the constitution of her species and of her sex in order to fill her place in the physical and moral order").[11] When Rousseau refers to the 'moral order,' or one's sense of oneself as a 'moral being,' he means the position one will hold in society, how one understands oneself in relationships with others. This is where '*pitié*' comes into play for men. Again, this *term* is not used in reference to women. Holding a position in the 'moral order' is "primarily a matter of recognizing oneself as, and as being recognized as, a bearer of rights . . . which equip one to enjoy a certain standing with others in society . . . It is to have a certain status, and to act in terms of one's possession of that status."[12] To *assume* 'moral being,' that is, understanding one's duties to others in society, as well as one's relationship with others, is, for Rousseau, a crucial element in the domestic education of females from birth. (Rousseau's proposed domestic education for males places this part of socialization at the point of puberty). Rousseau emphatically proclaims that woman's status in the moral order (Rousseau makes no distinction between the moral order, the social order, and the political order) is motherhood, and it is "par des loix générales que la nature et les mœurs doivent pourvoir à cet état"[13] ("by general laws that nature and morals/manners must provide for this status"). Woman's *civil* rights are a mother's rights. The relationship between woman's body and her moral/social/political being is clarified in what follows.

In order to distinguish between the sexes, Rousseau first tells us the constitution of woman's species. In everything *not* connected with sex, "la femme est homme" ("woman is man").[14] This will be a description of the common physical characteristics of the male and female bodies. The body of man is the model for the human body. Thus, in the following ways, 'woman' is *human*. Woman and man have *some* of the same internal organs (e.g., heart, lungs, stomach, liver, etc.) and the same basic needs (food, clothing, shelter, sex). The parts of woman's body (arms, legs, feet, hands, and head) are the same as the parts of man's body, and these parts function in the same way for woman as they do for man. The form of woman is *similar* to the form of man. Rousseau says that "sous quelque rapport qu'on les considére, ils ne différent entre eux que du plus ou moins"[15] ("in whatever relation one considers them, the only difference between them is that of more or less"). For example, Rousseau says that "Toutes les facultés communes aux deux séxes ne leur sont pas également partagées, mais prises en tout elles se compensent"[16] ("All the faculties common to the two sexes are not equally divided/shared, but taken together they balance"). These *"facultés"* refer to physical abilities, *perfectibilité*, and metaphysical liberty (for Rousseau, this means free will). In addition, both woman and man possess the faculty of judgment (or taste), but in different ways. Rousseau says,

> Consultez le goût des femmes dans les choses physiques et qui tiennent au jugement des sens, celui des hommes dans les choses morales et qui dépendent plus de l'entendement. Quand les femmes seront ce qu'elles doivent être elles se borneront aux choses de leur compétence et jugeront toujours bien.[17]
>
> Consult the judgment of women in those things physical and connected to the judgment of the senses, that of men in those things moral and dependent more on understanding. When women are what they must be they will confine themselves to the things within their competence and always judge well.

In the original and natural states, males and females are governed by three action-guiding passions, or instincts (inclinations, or dispositions). In Book IV of *Émile*, Rousseau explains that "Nos passions sont les principaux instruments de nôtre conservation"[18] ("Our passions are the principle instruments of our conservation"). The three *natural* passions are *amour de soi* (the individual), *pitié* (the social/political), and physical *amour* (the sex drive; the interpersonal).

In its primitive form, *amour de soi* means, roughly, self-preservation, the preservation of one's body and life. In the civil state, Rousseau modifies the definition of this term. This is the passion Rousseau suggests should be cultivated first in males. In Book IV of *Émile*, Rousseau explains that:

> La source de nos passions, l'origine et le principe de toutes les autres, la seule qui naît avec l'homme et ne le quitte jamais tant qu'il vit est l'amour de soi; passion primitive, innée, antérieur à toute autre et dont toutes les autres ne sont en un sens que des modifications.[19]
>
> The source our passions, the origin and the principle of all the others, the only one born with man and which never leaves him as long as he lives is *amour de soi*; a primitive passion, innate, anterior to all others and of which all the others are in a sense only modifications.

Rousseau says that in order to preserve ourselves, we must love ourselves, and from this it follows that we love that which preserves us. From *amour de soi* the faculties of attack and defense are born. Rousseau explains that what fosters the well-being of an individual attracts that individual; that which threatens harm repels the individual. Thus, one will defend oneself against actual or potential harm. Rousseau says that "Ce qui nous sert, on le cherche, mais ce qui nous veut servir, on l'aime; ce qui nous nuit, on le fuit, mais ce qui nous veut nuire, on le hait" [20] ("That which serves us, we seek, but we love that which wants to serve us; that which harms us, we flee, but we hate that which wants to harm us"). With regard to the relationship between the sexes, a man will only love a woman who wants to serve him, preserve his happiness, his patrimony (i.e., wealth), etc. In the civil state, this passion also refers to the preservation of man's individual liberty (freedom from external constraints on his actions and independence from the will, opinions, and judgments of others). Rousseau does mention the faculties of attack and defense with regard to the sexual relations between spouses and he discusses preserving woman's status in society, but *not* her individual liberty. Moreover, woman must *want* to serve man, to preserve *him*.

The second natural passion is *pitié*, which generally means 'compassion,' a distaste for the suffering of beings like oneself. This is the second passion that should be cultivated in the male. *Pitié* takes man outside of himself, brings him into contact and relations with others. In the civil state, with regard to man, this passion also concerns man's relationship with other men in society. If *pitié* is cultivated, rather than believe himself to be superior because of some title or greater wealth, man will feel compassion and a sense of common humanity with those less fortunate. In his *Discours sur l'origine et les fondements de l'inégalité parmi les hommes*, Rousseau compares this passion to the actions of a mother when her child is in danger.[21] However, as stated earlier, neither sense of this term is applied to 'woman' in Book V of *Émile*. Again, as stated earlier, *pitié* concerns an attitude towards *beings like oneself*. This concerns the social/moral/political relations between *men*. Woman's social/moral/political relation with *a* man is discussed in terms of duty, not *pitié*.

The third *natural* passion is physical *amour*. With regard to the relationship between the sexes, and specifically with regard to woman's dominant action-guiding principle, Rousseau always uses the term '*l'amour*' in reference to the *act* of love, sexual intercourse. In his *Discours sur l'origine et les fondements de l'inégalité parmi les hommes*, Rousseau says,

> Parmi les passions qui agitent le cœur de l'homme, il en est une ardente, impétsteuse, qui rend un sexe necessaire à l'autre, passion terrible qui brave tous les dangers, renverse tous les obstacles, et qui dans ses fureurs semble propre à détruire le Genre-humain qu'elle est destinée à conserver.[22]
> Among the passions which agitate the heart of man, is in him one ardent, impestuous; which renders one sex necessary to the other, a terrible passion that

braves all dangers, overturns all obstacle, and which in its furies seems likely to destroy Humankind which it is destined to preserve.

Rousseau provides a similar description of sexual passion in Book IV of *Émile* in his account of male puberty. Apparently, for males, puberty is a moment of crisis. Rousseau never discusses what puberty and sexual desire are like for women. For men, the sexual passion is a terrible thing!

Rousseau explains that physical *amour* is merely the general desire for sexual intercourse. This physical aspect of *amour* moves one sex to unite with the other (it guides action). Rousseau was concerned about this type of *amour* in his own time. The common sexual exploits of the upper class, in his opinion, threatened to destroy society.

In addition to *amour propre* (discussed earlier), there is one other artificial passion that is of importance in understanding Rousseau's theoretical account of 'woman', namely moral *amour*. Moral *amour*, according to Rousseau, is a social construct, born of social practice, "et célebré par les femmes avec beaucoup d'habilété et de soin pour établir leur empire, et rendre dominant le séxe qui devriot obéir"[23] ("and celebrated with much cleverness/skill and care by women in order to establish their empire/power and to make dominant the sex which must/ought to obey"). When Rousseau says in his *Lettre à d'Alembert* that "L'amour est le règne des femmes"[24] ("Love is the kingdom/reign of women"), he means sexual intercourse. This will be clear shortly. The moral aspect of *amour* focuses sexual desire on a particular *object* of desire, a *preferred object* of desire.

To recap, with regard to her species, woman is in some ways always a child, in some ways man, therefore, in some ways human (or, a human child). Woman possesses the characteristics of metaphysical liberty (free will) and *perfectibilité*, physical abilities, (woman is as capable as man of plucking an apple from a tree), the faculty of judgment (although with regard to physical things, not those things that require understanding), woman, like man, possesses the action-guiding passion of *l'amour*, and the faculties of attack and defense, thus, in some sense, the action-guiding passion of *amour de soi* (with regard to preserving her social status).

Now, let us turn to Rousseau's account of woman's sex, which is sparse, to say the least. In everything that *is* connected with sex, and thus *not of the species* (and thus, not human), "la femme et l'homme ont partout des *rapports* et partout des *differences*"[25] ("woman and man are in every way *related* and in every way *different*"). Rousseau says that the difficulty in comparing the sexes, and thus the cause of a common error (assuming that woman is an imperfect man–a common claim in Rousseau's time), "vient de celle de déterminer dans la constitution de l'un et de l'autre ce qui est du sexe et ce qui n'en est pas"[26] ("comes from that of determining in the constitution of one and the other that which is [related to] sex and that which is not"). Rousseau says that comparative anatomy and simple observation reveal general differences between women and men that do not immediately *appear* to be related to sex. Rousseau does not elaborate on these differences. Insofar as we are comparing the female body and the male body from the onset of puberty, these differences may be obvious. For example, what can be *perceived* are facial differences, differences in the voices of the two sexes, and a difference in complexion. Physical differences include women's extended breasts. Of course, man has a penis and woman does not. Internally, well, we have the different reproductive organs. Rousseau assures us that these general differences *are* connected with sex, but we are not in a position to *perceive* these relations. We do not know the extent of these relations. Rousseau says,

> ... la seule chose que nous savons avec certitude est que tout ce qu'ils ont de commun est de l'espéce, et que tout ce qu'ils ont de différent est du séxe; sous ce double point de vüe nous trouvons entre eux tant de rapports et tant d'oppositions, que c'est peut-être une des merveilles de la nature d'avoir pu faire *deux êtres si semblables* in les constitution si différent.[27]
>
> ... the only thing that we know with certainty is that all that they have in common is of the species, and that everything that is different is of the sex; from this double point of view we find between them so many relations and so many oppositions, that it is perhaps one of the marvels of nature to have been able to make *two such similar beings* so different in their constitution.

Notice that this is the third time Rousseau has referred to woman and man as *similar* kinds of beings. While Rousseau denies that woman is an imperfect man, he appropriates the commonly held belief in his time that woman is a *different* kind of animal. This is also implied in his discussion of *pitié* in the original state. In his *Discours sur l'origine et les fondements de l'inégalité parmi les hommes*, Rousseau compares this passion to the actions of a mother when her child is in danger. Rousseau says,

> Je parle de la Pitié, disposition convenable à des êtres aussi foirbles, et sujets à autant de maux que nous le sommes: vertu d'autant plus universelle et d'autant plus utile à l'homme, qu'elle precede en lui l'usage de toute réflexion et si Naturelle que les Bêtes memes en donnent quelquefois des signes sensibles. *Sans parler de la tendresse des Mères pour leurs petits, et des perils qu'elles bravent, pour les en garantir.*[28]
>
> I speak of pity, a disposition suited to beings as weak and as subject to so many ills as we are; a virtue all the more universal and all the more useful to man as it precedes the exercise of all reflection in him and so Natural that the Beasts themselves sometimes show evident signs of it. *To say nothing of the tenderness Mothers feel for their young and of the dangers they brave in order to protect them.*

However, as stated earlier, neither sense of this term is applied to 'woman' in Book V of *Émile*. Again, as stated earlier, *pitié* concerns an attitude towards beings like oneself. This concerns one's social relations. Woman's place is *not* in the social realm.

It is these relations and these differences (i.e., woman's sex) that will determine woman's place in the moral order. Thus, what might appear to be an application of biological determinism is in actuality an application of social convention. Rousseau says that the fact that these relations and these differences *must* influence woman's place in the moral order is the *first consequence* of sex, and this "est sensible, conforme à l'experience, et montre la vanité des disputes sur la preference ou l'égalité des sexes"[29] ("is sensible [noticeable, obvious], consistent with experience, and shows the vanity of the disputes on the preference or the equality of the sexes"). Rousseau agrees with the modern natural law theorists of his day that "En ce qu'ils ont de commun ils ont égaux"[30] ("In that which they have in common they are equal"). For Rousseau, whether or not *this* equality should override the *inequalities* between the sexes in the civil state (which were defended on the basis of sex) is not an issue worthy of discussion. According to Rousseau, "en ce qu'ils ont de different ils ne sont pas comparables: une femme parfait et un homme parfait ne doivent pas plus ressembler d'esprit que de visage, et la perfection n'est pas susceptible de plus et de moins"[31] ("in that which they are different they are not comparable: a perfect woman and a perfect man must not resemble each other any more in spirit/mind/disposition than in looks, and perfection is not susceptible of [being] more or less"). Woman's '*esprit*,' her spirit, mind, wit, disposition, is *related* to, but *different* from, the spirit, mind, wit, and disposition of man. Insofar as everything concerning woman's sex is *not* of the species, it appears that woman's *mind* is not quite a *human* mind. Well, it must *not* be a human mind in the civil state. For Rousseau, equality and inequality have meaning only in reference to *the same kind of thing, or beings*. 'Woman' and 'man', in the civil state, are similar, but they are not the same kind of being. Woman and man have a common aim–procreation. However, woman's *particular* purpose in fulfilling *nature's* end–her purpose in accordance with the kind of being that she *must* be–is not the purpose of man. Man has duties and responsibilities that extend beyond the domestic sphere. Woman's duties and responsibilities, her purpose (motherhood) are restricted entirely to the home. 'Woman' is not less perfect than man because she does not resemble him more; she is perfect *for her kind*, she can *become* perfect for her kind, if she fulfills her proper purpose–if she is educated or socialized to fulfill her proper purpose.

ROUSSEAU'S SEXUAL POLITICS

Rousseau's next order of business is to explain the sexual relationship within marriage. It is here that we will learn the details of the power relations between the sexes. Let us see how woman and man influence the life, attitudes, and behavior of one another in the marital relationship.

Rousseau says that "Dans l'union des sexes chacun concourt également à l'objet commun, mais non pas de la même maniére"[32] ("In the union of the sexes each contributes equally to the common aim, but not in the same manner"). It is the *contribution* that is equal, not woman and man as contributors. The common *human* aim of woman and man is to procreate in order to preserve the species. As will become evident, one of woman's *duties* is to preserve the family. According to Rousseau, the purpose of the family is to preserve man's patrimony, or wealth.[33] *Man's* specific duty with regard to procreation (aside from the common aim of preserving the species and his duty to preserve his patrimony through legitimate heirs) is to society and the state. Man owes men to his species, he owes sociable men to society, and he owes citizens to the state.[34]

The different manner in which woman and man contribute to their common aim is important. What follows has been taken out of context by commentators and critics of Rousseau. Thus, the emphasis on the sexual relationship is not always recognized. In brief, man contributes the sperm, woman contributes the egg. Man gives, woman receives. We know how procreation takes place. This *different way of contributing* to the common aim is crucial in understanding Rousseau's sexual politics: "*De cette diversité nait la premiére différence assignable entre les rapports moraux d'un et de l'autre*"[35] ("*From this difference is born the first assignable difference in the moral relations between the one and the other*"). It will be clear in what follows that Rousseau is talking about the moral *sexual* relations between the sexes. "L'un doit être actif et fort, l'autre passif et foible; il faut necessairement que l'un veuille et puisse; il suffit que l'autre resiste peu"[36] ("One must be active and strong, the other passive and weak; it is necessary that one will and be able; it is sufficient that the other offer little resistance"). A necessary condition is one that must exist if an event is to occur. Thus, man *must* will and desire, sexual intercourse, and man *must* be able to engage in sexual intercourse. That is, he must be physically capable, and the opportunity must be present. Moreover, woman must allow this to happen. A sufficient condition is one that guarantees that an event will occur. *If* woman puts up little resistance to man's sexual advances, sexual intercourse will occur. It is not necessary that a woman will and desire sexual intercourse. Moreover, although resistance is, according to Rousseau, a *certain* way of inciting man's passion (where there is no will or desire), sexual intercourse *can* take place without resistance in any degree.

This is a *second consequence* which Rousseau claims follows from the constitution of the sexes. Rousseau is not describing the day to day interactions between wives and husbands. He is describing sexual intercourse. What makes this act *moral* is that there is a specific object of desire (one's spouse). Otherwise, according to Rousseau, the *act* of sexual intercourse is the same regardless of whether it is purely physical or moral. It may be of use to bear in mind that in Rousseau's time, marital sex among the aristocracy (the group of interest for Rousseau) was not in fashion. It is going to be woman's duty to make marital sex occur. Moreover, it may seem as though I am focusing *only* on the sexual aspect of Rousseau's account of woman. Well, Rousseau seldom speaks of 'woman', or women, in any way that is *not* in reference to her sexuality - her sexual function, her sexual conduct, and her sexual charms. Rousseau compares and contrasts the sexual behavior of female human animals to the sexual behavior of non-human female animals. In brief, most of what Rousseau says about 'woman', women, and female children, is in reference to female sexuality.

From the diversity in the way woman and man contribute to the common aim of procreation *through sexual intercourse*, Rousseau claims that it immediately follows that "la femme est faite spécialement pour plaire à l'homme"[37] ("woman is made specially in order to please man"). This refers to woman as a social construct. If man must please woman, it is by a less direct necessity, "son *mérite* est dans sa *puissance*, il plait par cela seul qu'il est *fort*"[38] ("his *merit* [ability to please] is in his power [force, authority, control], he pleases solely by his strength"). Man's merit is his ability to please rather than his *right*, in this context, because Rousseau is arguing for mutual attraction. For Rousseau, 'authority' means "the rightful, legitimate title to command or require actions and forbearances from others."[39] Man's authority to command sexual actions from woman *is* his physical strength, and, Rousseau says, this is the law of nature.[40] Let us be very clear. Rousseau is not talking about man's physical attractiveness. In order to be pleasing to a woman, a man must be able to overpower her with his physical strength. This ability is what is attractive to a woman.

Rousseau continues with the claim that if woman is "faite pour plaire et pour être subjuguée"[41] ("made in order to please and in order to be subjugated"), she must render herself, *make* herself, agreeable to man–she must make herself accessible–rather than inflame his desires. Notice the sly way in which Rousseau interjects the claim that woman is made to be *subjugated*. Remember, Rousseau is talking about what woman *must* be in the civil state, and being made to be pleasing and subjugated will be part of her domestic education. One is not born to be pleasing and subjugated; one can *become* pleasing and subjugated. Rousseau says that "Sa *violence* à elle est dans ses charmes"[42] ("Her *violence* is in her charms"), and it is with these charms that woman must compel man to find his physical strength, and to use it.

This term '*violence*' is significant. The two most often cited translations of Rousseau's *Émile* are those of Allan Bloom and Barbara Foxley. Bloom provides a direct translation, retaining the term '*violence.*' Foxley, on the other hand, translates the term as 'strength,' which is the same term Foxley uses in translating '*puissance*' and '*fort.*' Man's "*puissance*" refers to *his* power, authority, and control over woman's body, behavior, and attitudes. Man's "*fort*" (force) refers to his physical strength. Man *pleases* woman in his physical ability to *take* her in sexual intercourse. The term '*violence*' is defined as "violence . . . an act of violence."[43] This term is used to refer to cases of verbal, physical, or sexual abuse, force, to "do violence to; violate; intense . . . rape."[44]

Recall that for Rousseau, 'power' means the capacity to change the life, attitudes and behavior of another. The change produced by woman's power, which is sexual, is that *she orchestrates and permits her own rape* within the marital relationship. Rousseau says that this is only *simulated* rape/violence. In all cases of sexual intercourse, according to Rousseau,

> Soit donc que la femelle de l'homme partage ou non ses désirs et veuille ou non les satisfaire, elle le repousse et se défend toujours, mais non pas toujours avec la même force ni par conséquent avec le même succès; pour que l'attaquant soit victorieux, il faut que l'attaqué le permette ou l'ordonne; car que de moyens adroits n'a-t-elle pas pour forcer l'agresseur d'user de force?[45]
>
> Whether the female of man [his wife] shares his desires or not and wants to satisfy them or not, she always repulses him and defends herself, but not always with the same force or consequently with the same success; in order for the attacker to be victorious, it is necessary for the attacked to permit or arrange it; for does she not have enough adroit [clever] means to force the aggressor to use force?

Rousseau says that although what is "plus doux pour l'homme dans sa victoire est de douter si c'est la foubless qui céde à la force ou si c'est la volonté qui se rend"[46] ("most pleasant for man in his victory is the doubt [as to] whether it is weakness which surrenders to force or if it is the will which surrenders"), it is a common ruse of women to let men wonder. However, "Le plus libre et le plus doux de tous les acts n'admet point de violence réelle"[47] ("The freest and most pleasant of all acts does not admit of real violence"). Rousseau says that real rape is in opposition to both nature and reason. Rape is opposed to nature because "la nature . . . a pourvu le plus foible d'autant de force qu'il en faut pour resister quand il lui plait"[48] ("nature . . . has provided the weakest with enough strength to resist when it pleases her"). Real rape is opposed to reason because not only is it the most brutal of all acts, but the act most contrary to its end. Either man declares war on woman and thereby gives her authority to defend her body and her *liberty* (here Rousseau means metaphysical liberty, or free will) even at the expense of his life (which implies that she has been given authority over man's body–she could kill him), or because she alone is the judge of her condition. If she should become pregnant, she alone knows whether or not that child is legitimate. No child would have a legitimate father if every man could usurp the rights of a father (the right to legitimate offspring). A common claim made by women attempting to file for divorce in the eighteenth century (a right granted to women only in extreme cases of abuse) was that they had been raped by their husbands, that is, marital rape. This notion that a husband can rape a wife was not generally accepted in our own society until the twentieth century, and there are still those who claim marital rape cannot occur. Although Rousseau is arguing for mutual attraction, he indirectly asserts man's right over woman's body. The age-old belief that sexual intercourse is a husband's right and a woman's duty is still alive and well. Other women, caught in the act of adultery, claimed they had been raped. Rousseau argues that, in his time, in Parisian high society, rape no longer took place (at least in cities). It was not necessary, since women made themselves readily available to men. Rousseau does say that in cases of great age disparity (a much older husband–remember, young girls were married at puberty, often to much older, and previously unknown, men) rape can occur. However, Rousseau thinks this is rare.[49] It is worth noting a problem with Rousseau's account of the rarity of rape and the ubiquity of (apparent) force. It would be impossible to tell the difference between rape and non-rape. Thus Rousseau's claim that rape is a rare occurrence, or that rape occurs at all, is unwarranted. How would he know?

Woman's dominant action-guiding passion is, and must be *amour*. From the sexual union are born the faculties of attack and defense–faculties of self-preservation, *amour de soi*. It is woman's *social status* and her lifestyle, not her individual liberty, that will be preserved. It is also through their reproductive function that women will preserve their status in society. Attack and defense are, Rousseau maintains, the most certain art of animating man's strength and compelling him to make use of that strength. Then, man triumphs in the victory that woman has forced him to win.[50] From this artistic, simulated rape arises the boldness of man, the timidity of woman, and "la modestie et la honte dont la nature arma le foible pour asservir le fort"[51] ("the modesty and shame with which nature armed the weak in order to enslave the strong"). What about this modesty and shame Rousseau speaks of? Why is this necessary? Here we will see Rousseau explicitly gender Plato's "noble lie."

Rousseau explains that, unlike other female animals, woman's sexual desires are not cyclical–they are ongoing and unlimited. Woman does not possess the natural instinct of other female beasts which, for them, serves as a brake on sexual desire. If woman does not have this *"pudeur,"* this sexual modesty, what will control her sexual urges? Rousseau says, "Attendre qu'elles ne se soucient plus des hommes, c'est attendre qu'ils ne soient plus bons à rien"[52] ("To wait until they no longer care for men, is to wait until they are no longer good for anything"). Well, what woman is good for is quite clear. Rousseau does not want to eliminate woman's sexual passions, he merely wants to control them. The claim that woman's power is in her sexual charms was another commonly held belief in Rousseau's time, and still common in the present.[53] This "natural" modesty and shame are joined to woman's unlimited sexual desires, by the Supreme Being, so that woman can *constrain* her passion. In man, the Supreme Being joins *reason* with man's sexual inclinations so that man can *govern* them. Thus, nature and the Divine have joined forces to control women's sexual conduct.[54]

It is irrelevant to Rousseau whether or not this modesty and shame are *really* natural and/or endowed by the Supreme Being. Rousseau offers a justification for the need for women to believe that they possess this sexual modesty and shame:

> Quand on pourrait nier qu'un sentiment particulier de pudeur fût naturel aux femmes, en serait-ils moins vrai que, dans la société, leur partage doit être une vie domestique et retirée, et qu'on doit les élever dans des principes qui s'y rapportent? Si la timidité, la pudeur, la modestie qui leur sont propres sont des inventions sociales, il importe à la société que les femmes aquièrent ces qualities; il importe de les cultivar en elles, et toute femme qui les dédaigne offense les bonnes mœurs.[55]
>
> Even if one might deny that a particular sentiment of chasteness was natural to women, would it be any less true that, in society, their lot must be a domestic and retired life, and that one must raise them with principles in keeping with it? If the timidity, chasteness, modesty which is proper to them are social inventions, it is of importance to society that women acquire these qualities; it is of importance to cultivate these [qualities] in them [women], and any woman who scorns them offends good morals.

Here again, we see Rousseau's appeal to social convention. Moreover, in this passage, Rousseau is giving us a heads-up with regard to the domestic education of women.

Rousseau has noted three consequences that he claims follow from the constitution of the sexes. The first consequence is that sex (differences in anatomy, mind, wit, and guiding passions) influences the moral (sexual) relations between women and men. The second consequence is that one, man, must be active and strong, the other, woman, must be passive and weak; it is necessary that man will and be able, it is sufficient that woman put up little resistance (just enough to animate man's strength).

The *third consequence* of the constitution of the sexes is that "le plus fort soit le maitre en apparence et depend en effet du plus foible"[56] ("the stronger appear to be the master and in effect depend on the weaker"). This, Rousseau maintains, is "une invariable loi de la nature, qui, donnant à la femme plus de facilité d'exciter les desirs qu'à l'homme de les satisfaire, fait dépendre celui-ci malgré qu'il en ait du bon plaisir de l'autre, et le contraint à le laisser être le plus fort"[57] ("an invariable law of nature, which, giving woman more facility to excite desires than man to satisfy them, makes the latter depend on her wishes and compels him to please her whether he likes it or not, so she will consent to let him be stronger"). Woman's *civil* rights, the rights owed to her by the state, are the rights of a mother. Woman's right within the marital relationship, is "le droit d'être foibles au besoin"[58] ("the right to be weak as need be").

Rousseau has taken us from the physical to the moral, and shown us how the most pleasing laws of love are born of the coarse sexual union of woman and man. Woman's empire, her domain, her realm of power (influence) is the sexual relationship. In addition to power through sexual intercourse, women possess a special, superior, talent that allows them to govern men while obeying at the same time. This special talent is flirting. Rousseau gives an account of a little girl who wanted to eat a dish she had not yet sampled. Rousseau says that, after being asked whether she wanted more of every other dish she had sampled, someone finally asked if she had tried the very dish she *wanted* to sample. Rousseau reports that the little girl was "doucement . . . baissant les yeux"[59] ("sweetly . . . lowering her eyes"). This "ruse" is a particular talent of females. Rousseau says that "La femme a tout contre elle, nos défauts, sa timidité, sa foublesse; elle n'a pour elle que son art et sa beauté"[60] ("Woman has everthing against her, our defects [shortcomings], her timidity, her weakness; she has nothing in her favor except her art and her beauty"). Woman's wit, her art, is in her sexuality and using her charms, for example flirting. Beauty is accidental, and try as one might, one may not be able to cultivate what society considers beauty in a woman. However, the art of flirtation can, and must, be cultivated. It is beneficial to woman. She can exploit man's position in society and put men's privileges to her own use.

Rousseau says that women's possession of their empire (their sexual kingdom) is not because *men* want it that way, "mais parce qu'ainsi le veut la nature"[61] ("but because nature wants it [that way]"). Rousseau says that even Samson was no match for Delilah's sexual charms. This empire belongs to women and cannot be taken from them, even when women abuse their sexual power. If women *could* lose their empire, their kingdom, they would have lost it long ago. Whether it is a flirtatious child, a virtuous wife, or a temptress, the power of the female is sexual. The next order of business, in Rousseau, is to establish the duties of woman in the civil state.

WOMAN'S DUTIES

Rousseau says that "Il n'y a nulle parité entre les deux séxes quant à la consequence du sexe"[62] ("There is no equality between the sexes with regard to the consequences of sex"). Man is a *gendered* male only part of the time–when he is engaged in sexual intercourse, being a proper father and husband, fulfilling his duties to the state or in his interactions with other men. There are times when man is an individual, on his own, with no responsibilities. Woman, however, is *gendered* 'woman' her entire life–or at least in her childbearing years. Everything reminds her of her sex. In order to fulfill the functions of her sex (procreation, preserving the family), she needs care during pregnancy, rest at the time she gives birth, a sedentary and easy life so that she may breastfeed without stress and anxiety. Woman needs patience, enthusiasm for her duty, and an affection for her child (which, according to Rousseau, develops through the habit of caring for one's child–through breastfeeding the bond between mother and child is formed). Woman serves as the emotional link between a man and his children. She alone makes a man love his children and assures him that they are his legitimate offspring. It is her *duty* to preserve the unity of the entire family.

The strictness of the relative duties of the sexes "n'est ni ne peut être la meme"[63] ("is not and can not be the same"). In response to complaints by women in his time concerning the unjust inequality between the sexes in the marital relationship, Rousseau says that these are not inequalities based on *prejudice*, but on *reason* (acceptable inequalities for Rousseau). Rousseau's explanation for the inequality between the sexes with regard to their duties is that it is up to women, the sex that nature charged with bearing children, to be accountable for the legitimacy of those children to the other sex, to men. Here, Rousseau is going to address the issue of adultery. Rousseau says that "Sans doute il n'est permis à persone de violer sa foi, et tout mari infidelle qui prive sa femme du seul prix des austéres devoirs de son séxe est un homme injuste et barbare"⁶⁴ ("Without doubt it is not permitted to anyone to violate his faith [oath], and every unfaithful husband who deprives his wife of the only prize for the austere duties of her sex is an unjust and barbarous man"). Woman's *prize*, her reward for her austere duties, is a faithful husband! As bad as it may be for a husband to commit adultery, "la femme infidelle fait plus, elle dissout la famille, et brise tous les liens de la nature; en donnant à l'homme des enfans qui ne sont pas à lui elle trahit les uns et les autres, elle joint perfidie à infidélité"⁶⁵ ("the unfaithful wife does more, she dissolves the family, and breaks all the bonds of nature; in giving to man children that are not his she betrays one and the other, she unites treason [breach of faith/trust/vows] with infidelity"). The double-standard in the eighteenth century considered adultery committed by a woman to be an act of treason. Once again, Rousseau is not making a startling claim to his audience. This was the law. Rousseau says, "J'ai peine à voir quel désordre et quel crime ne tient pas à celui-là"⁶⁶ ("I have difficulty seeing what disorder and what crime does not derive from this one"). It is agreed among interpreters that, for Rousseau, woman is the root cause of all social disorders. Here, we have clarification–it is woman's uncontrolled sexual conduct that is the root of all disorders.

For these reasons, Rousseau says, it is important not only that a woman *be* faithful, but that she be *judged* as faithful by her husband, by those who are around her in the community, "par tout le monde"⁶⁷ ("by everyone"). Thus, in addition to her first duty (motherhood), her duty to orchestrate sexual intercourse, and her duty to preserve the unity of the family, woman has *the added duty of appearance*–the appearance of virtue. It is important that a father love his children. Rousseau does not think a man will have affection for children other than his own. If man is to love his children, he must respect their mother. Honor, reputation, and chastity are indispensable for woman.

Rousseau thinks that he has established that the constitutions of woman and man are not, and must not be the same in either character or temperament. Thus, it follows, according to Rousseau, that the domestic education (i.e., socialization) of the sexes must not be the same. Rousseau says that, with regard to the education of females, "Tout ce qui caractérise le sexe doit être respecté comme etabli par [la nature]"⁶⁸ ("Everything which characterizes the [woman's] sex must be respected as established by [nature]"). As stated earlier, it is irrelevant to Rousseau whether his account of woman's "nature" is true, or even what he believes to be true about female humans outside the civil state. The value of individual women is in their conformity to the social concept of 'woman.' Telling females "noble lies" about their nature is in their best interest (it will preserve their status and prepare them for their proper role in society), it will make men happy and virtuous, and it will benefit the state (by allowing men to fulfill their duty of providing the state with good citizens). It should be clear at this point that, in the civil state, and at least theoretically, woman has no intrinsic value for Rousseau. Her value is *only* in being 'woman.' How does a female become 'woman'? Rousseau explains how females should be educated.

THE EDUCATION OF 'WOMAN'

Woman's purpose, her duties, and her inclinations (her dominant action-guiding passion) determine the education best suited for females–so that they may *become* 'woman.' For Rousseau, 'woman' and 'man' are both social constructs. Man is "made" for women, and woman is "made" for men. This is not about a "soul-mate" connection. Women and men depend on each other in order to fulfill their common duties. This dependence is *not* mutual. Men depend on women for the satisfaction of their sexual desires and the desire for legitimate children. Women depend on men for the satisfaction of their sexual desires, "et par leurs besoins"[69] ("and for their needs"). Rousseau does not elaborate on these needs, but it appears that he is focused on woman's need to preserve her station in society. Moreover, woman depends on man to judge her as worthy of his esteem. Rousseau explains that men would survive more easily without women than women would survive without men. In Rousseau's time, there were no job opportunities for women of the aristocracy, and they were not educated for any type of profession. Aristocratic females were socialized to be wives. Women depend on men to give them what is necessary to their station, and women depend on men to *want* to give them what is necessary to their station, to consider them worthy of what they can only get from men. Women depend on men's sentiments, on the value men place on women's merit, and the importance men attach to women's sexual charms as well as their virtues. Here we have another "noble lie." Rousseau says that "Par la loi meme de la nature les femmes, tant pour elles que pour leurs enfans, sont à la merci des jugemens des hommes"[70] ("By the very law of nature women, as much for themselves as for their children, are at the mercy of the judgment of men"). Well, this is not really a lie insofar as, in terms of laws and ideology, this was a reality for women in his time. Rousseau is reiterating what he said with regard to woman's duty. In this section, being judged by men is going to form the foundation of the domestic education for women. It is not enough that woman *is* worthy of respect, she must *be* respected. It is not enough for women to *be* pretty, they must please men. It is not enough for women to *be* temperate, they must be *recognized* as temperate. Women must be taught that while the opinion of other men "est le tombeau de la vertu parmi les hommes, et son trône parmi les femmes"[71] ("is the grave of virtue among men, it is the throne among women").

Woman's *raison d'être*, the entire emphasis of the domestic education of women, must relate to men. Rousseau says,

> Leur plaire, leur être utiles, se faire aimer et honorer d'eux, les élever jeunes, les soigner grands, les conseiller, les consoler, leur rendre la vie agréable et douce, voila les devoirs des femmes dans tous les tems, et ce qu'on doit leur apprendre dès leur enfance. Tant qu'on ne remontera pas à ce principe on s'écartera du but, et tous les preceptes qu'on leur donnera ne serviront de rien pour leur bonheur ni pour le nôtre.[72]
>
> To please them, to be useful to them, to make herself loved and honored by them, to raise them when they are young, to care for them when they are grown, to counsel them, to console them, to make their lives agreeable and sweet, these are the duties of women in all times, and that which must be taught to them from childhood. As long as one does not return to this principle one will depart from the goal, and all the principles taught to women will be of no use to their happiness or to our own.

Again, Rousseau is claiming that it will be useful, for man *and* woman to educate females to be *for* men. Rousseau explains that, although every woman *wants* to please men, and every woman *must* want to, it is important that females learn to distinguish between a virtuous man and a rogue.

Adding to the "nature" of woman, Rousseau says that "La femme est coquette par état"[73] ("Woman is a coquette by her status"). Woman's status in the civil state is motherhood, which requires sexual intercourse. In order for sexual intercourse to occur, woman must be agreeable and pleasing, as well as recognized as such, to man. Women of the aristocracy were concerned with their appearance, adornments, clothes, male attention. This desire to be considered attractive to men is a useful desire. However, without proper guidance, woman's coquetry changes in its form and its object according to her views. Rousseau says that regulating these *views* according to those of nature will illuminate the education which suits females. What Rousseau means is that females shift the focus of their attention from one moment to the next. Rousseau explains how to accomplish this regulation. Little girls, Rousseau says, love adornments. This is exhibited in female children almost from birth. Little girls are not satisfied with merely *being* pretty, they want others to think they are pretty. It makes no difference *who* thinks the little girl is pretty–just anyone. For Rousseau, female children must be taught to be selective with regard to *who* perceives them as pretty. This is linked to Rousseau's distinction between physical and moral *amour*. If, as a child, the female is happy with just anyone's appraisal of her, she will not be inclined to limit the use of her sexual charms, and sexual encounters, to just one man. The first lesson for a girl is to develop physical attractiveness, to make herself desired and marketable–a coquette. However, according to Rousseau, it is important to regulate the female's desire to be perceived as pretty by *everyone*.

Rousseau provides another account of little girls. Rousseau tells us to observe a little girl playing with her doll. She dresses and undresses the doll repeatedly, looking for new combinations of adornments. Rousseau says that woman's natural inclination reveals itself in the child playing with her doll. The female child, claims Rousseau, awaits the time when *she* will be a doll–when she will be perceived as pretty. As she plays with her doll, the little girl is unaware of the passage of time, "elle n'en sait rien"[74] ("she knows nothing in/of it" or "she is unaware of it"). She only awaits the time when *she* will be perceived by a man as a doll. In *The Reign of Women in Eighteenth-Century France*, Vera Lee says that for a young noblewoman, "getting married meant being *someone* . . . only with marriage does she finally *become* someone."[75] For Rousseau, woman's value in society is only in relation to man. It is only when she is judged worthy by a man that she *becomes* a being of value. For Rousseau, the first lesson a female should focus on in her domestic education is making herself "marketable." Unless she is recognized by a man as worthy of his esteem, as a being of value to him, *she is nothing*. In the twentieth century, Penelope Russian's book entitled *Why Do I Think I Am Nothing Without A Man?* (1983) hit the bookstores. Well, from long before Rousseau into the present, women have been taught (through their domestic education, through the media, from society) that they *are* nothing without a man!

To sum up, Rousseau's domestic education for women places great emphasis on cultivating woman's sexual charms, physical attractiveness, perfecting the art of flirtation, learning to distinguish virtuous men from non-virtuous men (then using one's powers to be recognized and desired by a man of virtue). Females must be taught the utility of their education. Rousseau explains that unless women understand the utility, and unless their entrance into the marital relationship is perceived by women as an act of free will–women will not accept their duties and responsibilities. Explicit, physical coercion will not work. Depicting marital life as one of drudgery and missed opportunities is not going to restore virtue to women, and through women, to men and the state. Rousseau does not suggest changing any of the laws that were in place. Nor does he suggest attempting to change society's attitudes about 'woman' and women's place in the moral order. Rousseau is proposing a way to preserve the status quo for women in a way that will appeal to females.

I will conclude this Chapter by explaining to what extent Rousseau preserves, and makes possible, liberty for women. I will then bring to the forefront what may be obvious, but nonetheless important consequences for women in Rousseau's definition of 'woman,' his sexual politics, and his proposed domestic education for women, which was nothing new before Rousseau, in his own time, and into the present. Rousseau is merely more explicit in his descriptions and emphasis.

CONCLUDING REMARKS

'Woman', for Rousseau, possesses metaphysical liberty. If properly educated, women will voluntarily, by an act of free will, enter into the marital relationship and fulfill their duties in society. Rousseau thought that if women at least *believe* they have a choice in *who* they marry, they would be less inclined to be critical of marriage. In addition to what has already been stated, I will add that with regard to adultery and rape, women, Rousseau says, have enough physical strength to resist sexual advances *if they really want to*. Adultery is an act of free will. No one is to blame for the act other than the woman who fails to control her sexual passions. With regard to rape, this is also, in the end, an act of free will. If a woman *can* resist, but sexual intercourse takes place, then, for Rousseau, this is an indication that she really did not want to resist. In all fairness to Rousseau, he is discussing women's claims of marital rape and the claim of rape to excuse promiscuity. Although adulterous affairs were common among the aristocracy, the laws that allowed men to divorce their adulterous wives were still in place, and could be enforced at any time. Women could lose their social status and be left with no economic support at all if a husband decided he wanted to divorce on grounds of adultery. Rousseau's issue is that women used the claim of rape to retain their status and excuse their promiscuous behavior. Moreover, it is important to remember that the women Rousseau is addressing are the aristocratic women of Paris. Whether in most marriages or in adulterous affairs, Rousseau considered the charge of rape to be an unacceptable excuse for women to seek divorce or explain their sexual misconduct. Through acts of free will, women entered into sexual liaisons, and if women really did not want to engage in sexual relations with their husbands (or any man), they had enough strength to resist.

In addition to metaphysical liberty, for Rousseau, there is moral liberty. This form of liberty concerns a relationship of mutual respect in the moral order. *If* women are properly educated, and *if* women take their proper place in society, fulfill their duties–especially the duty of not only *being* virtuous, but of *appearing* virtuous to her husband and society–they *will* be respected by others *as a woman*. For Rousseau, mutual respect and affection between spouses is the ideal. If women are what they must be, they will be respected in the marital relationship. Women will respect men who are as they must be. This type of liberty is possible for women.

A third sense of liberty is civil liberty. This refers to the rights one is granted by the state. Rousseau suggests one change in this area in his literary works–he grants women at least the semblance of choosing *who* they will marry. In his theoretical treatise, however, this right is not granted to women. Women, in Rousseau have a mother's rights, but he does not provide the details of these rights, other than to mention the mother's right to her children's affection. In Rousseau's time, it was acceptable for widows to inherit. In a footnote in Book I of *Émile*, Rousseau mentions that it is quite common that a widow is dependent upon her children. Just because widows *could* inherit did not mean that they always *did*. Rousseau implies that a mother's rights include being taken care of if she is widowed and/or in her old age. For the most part, Rousseau's comments in his theoretical treatise are a denial of the rights women wanted–equal formal education, equal rights within the marriage, particularly the right to divorce (which Rousseau never mentions), basically any civil liberties extended to men but denied to women. Rousseau does not argue against a widow's right to inherit, thus we might assume that this civil liberty is preserved. Basically, with regard to civil liberty, Rousseau advocates preserving the status quo.

The form of liberty that Rousseau considered the most important, and which held the highest value, is individual liberty. Rousseau uses two senses of this form of liberty. On the one hand, individual liberty refers to one's ability and opportunity to carry out chosen acts or engage in projects without being constrained by external obstacles, lack of resources, or inadequate skills. Rousseau says that women's individual liberty must be limited, given that women tend to excess in everything that they do.[76] Women are economically and materially dependent upon men. Women are not taught job skills, nor should they be, according to Rousseau. Laws and women's upbringing prohibited opportunities. Economic and material liberty is not possible for women in Rousseau.

The second sense of individual liberty (and the most important sense for this project) concerns *internal* constraints, being dependent upon the opinions and judgments of others. I have explained that Rousseau makes women dependent upon men for their self-esteem, their sense of value, and even for the awareness of their own existence. This imposes a psychological constraint on women. This liberty is also denied to women. In the end, women possess metaphysical liberty and if properly educated, moral liberty. It seems that women may retain the few civil liberties they had in Rousseau's time. This is not clear.

Finally, I will address what may be obvious, but nonetheless important consequences for women in Rousseau's theoretical account of 'woman.' One consequence, raised earlier, is that women do not develop compassion. This is a "natural" action-guiding passion. Of course, we already know that Rousseau partially dehumanizes woman in the civil state. Moreover, woman is never considered as an individual in Rousseau. Woman's emphasis must be with regard to what is beneficial to the state, to man, to her children, and finally (almost as an afterthought), herself. But, the benefits to herself are *only* with regard to social status. Granted, the aristocratic woman in Rousseau's time had few options, preserving her status also preserved her economic security. However, in excluding the cultivation of compassion in his theoretical treatise, Rousseau adds to the dehumanization of woman (Rousseau does include this in his literary works; his literary heroines care for the ill and less fortunate. However, his fictional "ideal" women do not develop social relations outside of the family unit). To be considered only partially human reduces one's sense of dignity, and it justifies denying women equal rights and liberties.

Another, no doubt obvious, consequence of Rousseau's theoretical account of 'woman' is the sexual objectification of women in the marital relationship and in the state. Even more disturbing, however, is Rousseau's sexual objectification of little girls. It is eerie to read Rousseau's discussions of little girls and his emphasis on their sexuality. Teaching a child to make herself a sexual object, to cultivate her sexual charms, and to be concerned with how pretty she is–according to the judgments of others–reminds one of the "kiddie beauty pageants" of today. For the most part, Rousseau observed women and little girls of the aristocracy in his time, attributed their actions to "nature," recognizing all the while that they had been socialized, and simply tries to regulate that. This does not make it easier to think of Rousseau's account of little girls and the awareness that his proposed domestic education (which again, was not new, just more explicit) makes sexual objects of female children *and* women.

Although Rousseau is correct in the benefits for women in his time, the negatives outweigh the positives. Woman, in Rousseau, is partially dehumanized and sexually objectified. Moreover, the notion that woman must orchestrate and permit simulated rape in the marital relationship is demeaning and quite disturbing, and effectively disables women from *proving* rape.

While this Chapter may have become a bit tedious, it is important to understand the exact components of Rousseau's sexual politics, his definition of 'woman,' and how he advises mothers to socialize their daughters. In Chapter II, I will clarify Rousseau's ultimate philosophical project and show that his sexual politics is consistent with, even essential to, that project.

NOTES

1. Dent, N. J. H. *A Rousseau Dictionary*. Cambridge: Blackwell Publishers, 1992, p. 195.
2. Beauvoir, Simone de. *Le deuxième sexe, II*. Paris: Gallimard, 1949/1976, p. 13. The irony of this quote is that Beauvoir and Rousseau both claim that one *becomes*, or *can* become 'woman', however, they disagree as to what that *becoming* must be. Rousseau will argue tha 'woman' must be dependent, subjugated, deprived of individual, economic, material, intellectual, and psychological liberty. Beauvoir will argue that 'woman' must be independent, liberated, and free (economically, materially, intellectually, and psychologically).
3. Rousseau, Jean-Jacques. *Émile ou De l'éducation*. Paris: Gallimard, 1969, p. 325, my italics.
4. Ibid., p. 331.
5. Dent, p. 190.
6. Rousseau, Jean-Jacques. *Discours sur l'origine et les fondements de l'inégalité parmi les hommes*. Paris: Gallimard, 1969, p. 72.
7. Rousseau, *Émile*, 537.
8. Ibid.
9. Ibid.
10. Ibid.
11. Ibid., p. 528. Rousseau begins the sentence with reference to his fictional heroine Sophie. However, interpreters agree that in this instance, Sophie is representative of women in general. The specific character does not appear in this section of Book V of *Émile*, but reappears when Rousseau shifts from his theoretical account of woman back to his literary illustration of his "ideal" woman.
12. Dent, p. 164.
13. Rousseau, *Émile*, p. 535.
14. Ibid., p. 528.
15. Ibid.
16. Ibid., p. 537.
17. Ibid., p. 508.
18. Ibid., p. 326.
19. Ibid., p. 327.
20. Ibid., p. 328.
21. Rousseau, *Discours*, p. 85.
22. Ibid., p. 87.
23. Ibid., p. 88.
24. Rousseau, Jean-Jacques. *Lettre à d'Alembert*. Paris: Garnier-Flammarion, 1967, p. 113.
25. Rousseau, *Émile*, p. 529, my italics.
26. Ibid.
27. Ibid., my italics.
28. Rousseau, *Discours*, p. 84, my italics.

29. Ibid.
30. 30. Ibid.
31. Ibid.
32. Rousseau, *Émile*, p. 529.
33. Rousseau, Jean-Jacques. *Sur l'économie politique*. Paris: Flammarion, 1990, p. 58. According to Rousseau, the proper purpose of *all* women in the civil state is motherhood. However, if the purpose of the family is to preserve man's wealth, one might wonder at the point of poor people's marriages. Rousseau does not address this question in Book V of *Émile*. However, *all* men have a duty to preserve the species, provide men to society, and citizens to the state. Rousseau does not think that a man can form bonds of affection with illegitimate children. Moreover, in Rousseau's time, men had no legal obligation to provide for illegitimate children. In order to raise good men for society and the state, a man must care for his children. However, this does not explain the point of poor families. If one is poor, there is no patrimony to preserve. It is beyond the scope of this chapter, or this project, to fully explore this issue in Rousseau.
34. Rousseau, *Émile*, p. 98.
35. Ibid., p. 529, my italics.
36. Ibid.
37. Ibid.
38. Ibid., my italics.
39. Dent, p. 38.
40. Rousseau, *Émile*, p. 529.
41. Ibid.
42. Ibid., p. 530, my italics.
43. Collins *Robert French Dictionary*. New York: HarperCollins Publishers, 2002, p. 1078.
44. *Pocket French Dictionary*. New York: Langensheidt, 1992, p. 319.
45. Rousseau, *Émile*, p. 531.
46. Ibid., p. 532.
47. Ibid., p. 531.
48. Ibid..
49. Ibid., p. 532.
50. Ibid., p. 530.
51. Ibid.
52. Ibid., p. 531
53. Two historical sources that specifically discuss Rousseau and the social attitudes towards women in his time are Vera Lee's *The Reign of Women in Eighteenth-Century France* (Cambridge: Schenkman Publishing Company, 1975) and Mary Seidman Trouille's *Sexual Politics in the Enlightenment: Women Writers Read Rousseau* (New York: State University of New York Press, 1997).
54. Rousseau, *Émile*, pp. 530-531.
55. Rousseau, *Lettre à d'Alembert*, p. 175.
56. Rousseau, *Émile*, p. 531.
57. Ibid., pp. 531-532.

58. Ibid., p. 532.
59. Ibid., p. 548.
60. Ibid.
61. Ibid., p. 533.
62. Ibid.
63. Ibid.
64. Ibid.
65. Ibid., p. 534.
66. Ibid.
67. Ibid.
68. Ibid., p. 537.
69. Ibid., p. 538.
70. Ibid.
71. Ibid., p. 539.
72. Ibid.
73. Ibid.
74. Ibid., p. 542.
75. Lee, Vera. *The Reign of Women in Eighteenth-Century France.* Cambridge: Schenkman Publishing Company, 1975, pp. 9 and 15, respectively.
76. Rousseau, *Émile*, p. 546.

Chapter II

The Other Side of the Paradox

INTRODUCTION

Contemporary interpreters[1] of Rousseau's sexual politics disagree on four key points: (1) Rousseau's philosophical orientation; (2) what Rousseau's philosophical project *is*; (3) how Rousseau's various works relate to his project; and (4) whether or not Rousseau's sexual politics is consistent with (i.e., reinforces) or contradictory to (i.e., undermines) his philosophical project. The aim of this Chapter is to clarify these key points (i.e., the other side of the paradox). Taken together, Chapter I and Chapter II will show that Rousseau's sexual politics is consistent with, even essential to, his philosophical project.

CONTEMPORARY INTERPRETATIONS

Nicole Fermon reads, and rewrites, Rousseau "in the voice of woman, in the feminine voice."[2] Fermon understands Rousseau's ultimate objective to be the recovery of the 'maternal image' for the state. According to Fermon, Rousseau's vision "is a reworking of an egalitarian ethos independent of the corruption of the ancients."[3] Fermon says that Rousseau's philosophical project is grounded in a "democratic community of autonomous persons united through mores and habits and through their common tasks in creating themselves as moral beings."[4] Fermon maintains that the self-sufficient, rural estate of Clarens, depicted in Rousseau's novel *La Nouvelle Héloïse*, is his illustration of equality, liberty, and community *for all*. Fermon argues that the marital relationship in *La Nouvelle Héloïse* contradicts Rousseau's theoretical treatise on 'woman' and the marital relationship depicted in Book V of *Émile*.

Fermon says that the family structure in this work is modeled after the eighteenth-century French aristocratic family, and Julie, Rousseau's heroine, illustrates the maternal mainstay of the family and the community. Fermon alleges that Rousseau's *Du contrat social* is "the construction of a 'common mother,' interchangeably called the 'common liberty' of the people."[5] On Fermon's reading of Rousseau, liberty "is possible if we recover the mother and keep her alive forever in the institution that is the state."[6] Moreover, according to Fermon, it is through their role as administrators of morality that women have power and equality in Rousseau. According to Fermon, women's physical existence as caring, nurturing mothers (in the family *and* the community) illustrates Rousseau's "ideal" of liberty. Thus, for Fermon, Rousseau's sexual politics reinforces (i.e., is consistent with) his philosophical project.

In *The Sexual Politics of Jean-Jacques Rousseau*, Joel Schwartz reads Rousseau as a partial egalitarian. Schwartz agrees with Fermon that Rousseau's heroine Julie illustrates a feminist-friendly reading of Rousseau's views on the power relations between the sexes in marriage. However, Schwartz claims, this does not contradict Rousseau's account of the marital relationship in Book V of *Émile*. According to Schwartz, Rousseau's objective in his sexual politics as put forth in Book V of *Émile* is to establish *some* degree of equality between the sexes (to establish "equal and different"). Schwartz maintains that, in Rousseau's theoretical treatise, women are granted indirect but effectual power through the sexual interdependence of men and women. Moreover, Schwartz says that it is through sexual relations that *mutual* domination and subordination occurs. Schwartz claims that in Book V of *Émile*, "Rousseau wishes to argue that men and women are equal because of their differences,"[7] and this equality through sexual power allows women the *possibility* of attaining individual liberty (the most important and most valued sense of liberty for Rousseau). Schwartz admits that women's power and equality are limited to the marital relationship, and that women are "equals as wives and mothers (vis-à-vis husbands and fathers), but not as workers and citizens."[8] According to Schwartz, Rousseau's sexual politics is consistent with his philosophical project.

Penny A. Weiss says that "feminist commentaries condemning Rousseau's sexual politics . . . have called him an inconsistent liberal when he is not a liberal at all, consistent or otherwise."[9] Like Fermon, Weiss reads Rousseau as a communitarian, and also understands Rousseau's philosophical project to be illustrated in his novel *La Nouvelle Héloïse*. Weiss agrees with Schwartz that Julie illustrates women's indirect power through the sexual interdependence of men and women. However, contrary to Schwartz, Weiss maintains that this power is *ineffectual*. According to Weiss, "[a]lthough Rousseau resembles liberals in positing a condition – a state of nature – in which people are self-contained and separate, his belief that *each* distinctive environment ... shapes us, aligns him with feminists [in his attention to the range of forces that shape our identity] and communitarians."[10] In the end, Weiss concludes that, although Rousseau's views on women are "compatible with his general philosophical and political principles"[11] as put forth in *Émile* and *Du contrat social*, and illustrated in *La Nouvelle Héloïse,* Rousseau "fails to make the sexes equal and different, thus undermining his communitarian vision."[12] For Weiss, there is no internal consistency between Rousseau's sexual politics and his philosophical project.

Carole Pateman reads Rousseau as a social contract theorist (distinct from Hobbes and Locke), and understands his philosophical project to be his social contract as put forth in *Du contrat social*. Pateman maintains (contrary to Fermon's feminist reading) that Rousseau's social contract theory "cannot simply be revised to include women."[13] Moreover, Pateman contends, attempts to establish equality between the sexes through communitarian or egalitarian readings of Rousseau (contrary to Fermon, Schwartz, and Weiss) will fail because the problem is in the nature of social contracts and sexual contracts (i.e., marriage contracts). In addition, Pateman maintains that Rousseau's literary heroines, in both *Émile* and *La Nouvelle Héloïse* illustrate the stereotypical patriarchal housewife. According to Pateman, Rousseau's philosophical project (the social contract) and his sexual politics (the sexual/marriage contract as put forth in Book V of *Émile*) are mutually reinforcing. Pateman explains that "the sexual contract, the 'individual,' and the social contract, the 'state,' stand and fall together."[14] Pateman rejects attempts to appropriate Rousseau's philosophical project (the social contract) while rejecting his sexual politics as well as attempts at reconciling or resolving the paradox of Rousseau's sexual politics.[15] Thus, for Pateman, Rousseau's sexual politics is consistent with (even essential to) Rousseau's philosophical project, and there is no resolution to the paradox.

ROUSSEAU'S PHILOSOPHICAL ORIENTATION

Rousseau is not an egalitarian, communitarian, or a liberal – consistent or otherwise. I agree with Pateman's interpretation of Rousseau's philosophical orientation. However, I will add that Rousseau is a *natural law theorist*, sharing important similarities with *modern* natural law theory, but most closely aligned with *classical* nature law theory which is grounded in the philosophy of Aristotle (and still widely adhered to in Rousseau's time). Basic tenets of modern natural law theory that are evident in Rousseau include the belief in the natural liberty and equality of all human beings, and that human beings are naturally autonomous and self-governing.

Classical natural law theory is teleological, and has as its ground the tension between nature and convention. For Aristotle and Rousseau, the law of nature expresses the ends or purposes that by nature belong to a kind of living being. Human conventions, laws, and actions are right if they accord with the purposes of nature. This affinity with classical natural law theory is evident in Rousseau's theoretical treatise on 'woman' as explicated in Chapter I. This is further supported in the "Préface" to *Émile*, wherein Rousseau says, "En tout espece de projet, il a deux choses à considerer premierement, la bonté absolue du projet; en second lieu, la facilité de l'exécution"[16] ("In every sort of project, there are two principal things to consider: the absolute goodness of the project; secondly, the ease of its execution"). With regard to the first principal, Rousseau says, "il suffit, pour que le projet soit admissible et practicable en lui-même, que ce qu'il a de bon soit dans la nature de la chose"[17] ("it is sufficient, in order that the project may be acceptable and practicable in itself, that what is good in it may be in the nature of the thing"). Rousseau redefines woman's nature in the civil state, and thus, his proposed education for women is in accordance with woman's "nature." With regard to the second principal, Rousseau's identity politics, his sexual politics, his proposed domestic education for women, and his ideal marriage reflect the lifestyle of the *moyenne bourgeoisie* in his time. There is absolutely nothing new or original in Rousseau's theoretical treatise on woman. Rousseau is defending the patriarchal family, the traditional family, and advocating a return to this for the Parisian aristocracy and *haute bourgeoisie*.[18]

ROUSSEAU'S PHILOSOPHICAL PROJECT AND WORKS

Rousseau's ultimate philosophical project is the restoration of a sense of equality among men *as men*, the restoration of individual liberty (especially in the second sense discussed in Chapter I, that is, psychological independence) *to men*, the restoration of virtue *to men*, and the restoration of the family *to men* and *to the state*. Woman, in Rousseau's philosophical project, is necessary in the restoration of virtue, the family, and in man's attainment of individual (psychological) liberty (in the sense of being free of the judgments and opinions of women). The emphasis in contemporary interpretations of Rousseau is on equality and liberty, and either attempts to establish some degree of equality between the sexes and liberty for women, or to determine whether Rousseau's sexual politics undermines (i.e., contradicts) his notions of equality and liberty. In the literature, virtue is briefly mentioned or overlooked altogether.

In *Les Confessions*, Rousseau says that as he contemplated writing what became his *Discours sur les sciences et les arts*, for an essay contest, he experienced an enthusiasm for "la vérité, de la liberté, de la vertu"[19] ("truth, liberty, virtue") that remained with him for the subsequent four or five years. In those years, Rousseau also wrote *Discours sur l'origine et les fondements de l'inégalité parmi les hommes, Lettre à d'Alembert, La Nouvelle Héloïse, Émile,* and what came to be *Du contrat social.* Indeed, the key issues addressed in the discourses are repeated and/or rephrased in *Émile.*

The *Discours sur les sciences et les arts* is Rousseau's social criticism, his understanding of the fundamental problem *for men* in his time. This work addresses the loss of the sense of equality among men *as men*, the loss of individual liberty in that men were dependent on the opinions and judgments of others for their sense of self, value, and trying to be among the popular crowd. Women were especially influential in that they used their "feminine charms" to help make or break literary careers. This work also addresses the loss of virtue in terms of men's failure to fulfill their civil duties, behaving dishonestly with others, and in their moral conduct in general. In the *Discours sur l'origine et les fondements de l'inégalité parmi les hommes,* Rousseau traces the origins of these losses. *Émile* is Rousseau's proposed solution to the problem of his time. Books I-III explain how to instill in a male child the independence of others that is required for individual liberty in the most important sense for Rousseau. Book IV focuses on the transition from childhood to one's relations with other men in society, and establishes the sentiment of equality. Book V, as discussed in Chapter I, concerns the restoration of the family and virtue. This Book is about educating/socializing a virtuous woman.

With regard to women in Rousseau, virtue is the key concept. In the *Discours sur les sciences et les arts*, the only mention of women is in a footnote where Rousseau says, "Les hommes seront toûjours ce qu'il plaira aux femmes: si vous voulez donc qu'ils deviennent grands et vertueux, apprenez aux femmes ce que c'est que grandeur d'âme et vertu"[20] ("Men will always be what it pleases women that they be: if you want them to become great and virtuous, teach women what greatness of soul and virtue are").

Rousseau's "natural woman" in Book V of *Émile* is not a complete deviation from woman in the state of nature. For Rousseau, there are three states— the savage state, the natural state, and the civil state. *Natural* woman is the woman we find in the *Discours sur l'origine et les fondements de l'inégalité parmi les hommes,* when men, women, and children came together and took up residence in a common dwelling. Rousseau speculates (he never claims that this stage in human life actually happened) that the habit of living together "fit naître les plus doux sentimens qui soient connus des hommes, l'amour conjugal, et l'amour Paternel"[21] ("gave birth to the most pleasing sentiments known to man, conjugal love and Paternal love"). Each family formed its own society within a single dwelling, "et ce fut alors que s'établit la premiére difference dans la maniére de vivre des deux Séxes, qui jusqu'ici n'en avoient eu qu'une"[22] ("and that is when the first difference was established in the manner/ way of life of the two Sexes, which until then had had but one"). Prior to this point, the only difference in the way of life of the sexes was that the female could get pregnant and have to care for an infant. This is the lifestyle of the virtuous woman for Rousseau, sedentary and in the home.

Of the three ancillary works in progress, Rousseau's *Lettre à d'Alembert* is most closely aligned with his primary philosophical project. Like the *Discours sur les sciences et les arts*, this work is a social commentary/criticism of his time, addressing the negative effects of the theater on morals. His primary emphasis is the morality of women, and how women's moral conduct influences men. Rousseau makes statements reminiscent of his footnote in *Discours sur les sciences et les arts*. For example, Rousseau says, "Dans tout Etat, dans tout pays, dans toute condition, les deux sexes ont entre eux une liaison si forte et si naturelle que les mœurs de l'un décident toujours de celles de l'autre"[23] ("In every State, in every country, in every condition, the two sexes have between them a connection so strong and so natural that the morals of one always decides those of the other"). Lest we wonder whose morality is decided by the other, in *Émile*, Rousseau says that the morals of men "des femmes dependent"[24] ("depend on women"). In the *Lettre à d'Alembert*, Rousseau adds that "la vie des femmes est un développement continuel de leurs mœurs, au lieu que, celles des hommes s'effaçant dadvantage dans l'uniformité des affaires, il faut attendre pour en juger de les voir dans les plaisirs. Voulez-vous donc conaître les hommes? Etudiez les femmes"[25] ("the life of women is a continual development of their morals, whereas, since those of man wear away more in the uniformity of business, one must wait to see them in their pleasures to judge of them. Do you want to know men? Study women"). Another well-known comment about the morality of women in the *Lettre à d'Alembert* is that "Jamais peuple n'a péri par l'excès du vin, tous périssent par le désordre des femmes"[26] ("Never has a people perished by the excess of wine, all perish by the disorder of women"). The disorder of women is a *moral* disorder. Rousseau reiterates his comments about women's realm of influence (the sexual realm) and the idea of men forcing women to engage in sex when he says, "L'amour est le règne des femmes. Ce sont celles qui nécessairement y donnent la loi: parce que, selon l'ordre de la Nature, la résistance leur appartient et que les hommes ne peuvent vaincre cette résistance qu'aux dépens de leur liberté"[27] ("Love is the realm of women. It is they who necessarily make the law in it: because, according to the order of Nature, resistance belongs to them and men can conquer this resistance only at the expense of their liberty"). Recall that Bloom says Rousseau preserves man's free will without denying women their free will. This is how Rousseau accomplishes that feat.

There is a pattern in Rousseau's three principal works concerning his objectives for men that is mirrored in his objectives for women if we include the *Lettre à d'Alembert* as part of his principal works. The *Discours sur les sciences et les arts* illuminates what Rousseau considered to be the fundamental problem for men in his time; the *Discours sur l'origine et les fondements de l'inégalité parmi les hommes* locates the origin of the problem; and *Émile* proposes a solution. Shifting our focus to women, we find the fundamental problem *with* women in Rousseau's time in the *Lettre à d'Alembert*; we find comments on women's sexuality and adultery along with the origin of woman's "problem" in the *Discours sur l'origine et les fondements de l'inégalité parmi les hommes*; and we find the proposed solution in *Émile* and the aforementioned footnote in *Discours sur les sciences et les arts*.

Rousseau's other two works, *Du contrat social* and *La Nouvelle Héloïse* share common themes with Rousseau's principal works, but they are not part of his philosophical *project* and the principal works concerning that project. Rousseau can be approached in a variety of ways, and one can trace common themes in his works. However, these two works seem a bit out of place. *Within* the corpus of Rousseau's work, and in an attempt to adequately understand Rousseau on the issue of the relations between the sexes, other than reinforcing the exclusion of women from political participation, *Du contrat social* is of little use for a feminist reading of Rousseau. Rousseau was of the opinion that his proposed educations for women and men could be implemented, but he does not propose establishing the "ideal" state. He is merely suggesting the best state for the formation of virtuous women and men.

In *Les Confessions*, Rousseau explains he was working on various projects during his stay in the country in 1756. The work that most appealed to him initially was one entitled *Institutions politiques*. Rousseau adds:

> ... mes vues s'étaient beaucoup étendues par l'étude historique de la morale. J'avais vu que tout tenait radicalement à la politique, et que, de quelque façon qu'on s'y prit, aucun people ne serait jamias que ce la nature de son gouvernement le ferait être; ainsi cette grande question du meilleur gouvernement possible me paraissait se réduire à celle-ci: Quelle est la nature du gouvernement propre a former un people le plus vertueux, le plus éclairé, le plus sage, le meilleur enfin ... Je voyais que tout cela me menait a des grandes verités, utiles au bonheur du genre humane ...[28]
>
> ... my views/ideas had been greatly broadened by the study of the history of morals. I had seen that everything was radically rooted in the political, and that, however one might go about it, no people would ever be other than what

the nature of their government made them; so that great question of the best possible government seemed to me to reduce itself to this: What is the nature of the government suited to forming the most virtuous, the most enlightened, the wisest, in fact the best people . . . I saw that all that was leading me to some great truths useful for humanity . . .

Later, Rousseau says that he realized this work would require more time than he wanted to invest, thus, he abandoned this work, extracting whatever could be extracted, and burned the rest. Rousseau says that "sans interrompre celui de l'*Émile*, je mis, en moins de deux ans, la dernière main au *Contrat social*"[29] ("without interruption to *Émile*, I put, in less than two years, the finishing touches on the *Contrat social*"). As Rousseau wrote *Du contrat social*, he was not thinking of a movement from *Émile* to an ideal state. Rousseau's notions of civil equality and liberty can be appropriated (contrary to Pateman, and as I will show in Chapter IV), but within the corpus of Rousseau's work, *Du contrat social* excludes women from participation in the making and enforcing of laws, which is consistent with his sexual politics.

La Nouvelle Héloïse began as an imaginary group of friends created by Rousseau who was disillusioned with his acquaintances. Rousseau explains:

> J'imaginai deux amies plutôt que deux amis, parce que si l'exemple est plus rare, il est aussi plus aimable. Je les douai de deux caractères analogues, mais different; de deux figures non pas parfaits, mais de mon goût, qu'animaient la bienveillance et la sensibilité. Je fis l'une brune et l'autre blonde, l'une vive et l'autre douce, l'une sage et l'autre faible; mais d'une si touchante faiblesse, que la vertu semblait y gagner. Je donnai à l'une des deux un amant dont l'autre fut la tender amie, et meme quelque chose de plus; mais je n'admis ni rivalité ni querelle, ni jalousie, parce que tout sentiment pénible me coûte à imaginer, et que je ne voulais ternir ce riant tableau par rien qui dégradât la nature. Épris de mes deux charmants modeles, je m'identifiais avec l'amant et l'ami le plus qu'il m'était possible; mais je le fis aimable et jeune, lui donnant au surplus les vertus et les défauts que je me sentais.[30]

> I imagined two [women] friends, rather than two [men] friends, since although examples of such friendships are rarer they are also more enjoyable. I endowed them with two analogous but different characters; with two appearances not perfect yet to my taste, and radiant with kindliness and sensitivity. I made one dark-haired, the other blond; one lively, the other gentle; one sensible, the other weak, but so touching in her weakness that virtue itself seemed to gain by it. I gave one of them a lover to whom the other was a tender friend and even something more; but I allowed of no rivalry or quarrels or jealousy because I did not wish to tarnish my charming picture with anything degrading to nature. Captivated by my two charming models, I identified myself as much as I could with the lover and friend. But I made him pleasant and young, endowing him also with the virtues and faults that I felt in myself.

The first two parts of this novel were written in the form of scattered letters, with no real form or plan. In bad weather, confined to his house, Rousseau says that he found it difficult to think of anything except the "deux charmantes amies, que leur ami, leurs entours, le pays qu'elle habitaient, qu'objets créés our embellish pour elles par mon imagination"[31] ("two charming friends, their friend, their surroundings, and the country they lived in, nothing but objects created or embellished for them by my imagination"). Rousseau decided to control his obsession by creating some type of order for his imaginings and scattered bits of letters, and turn them into a novel. Finally sketching out a plan, Rousseau says, "l'amour du bien, qui n'est jamais sorti de mon cœur, les tourna vers des objets utiles, et don't la moral eût pu faire son profit"[32] ("the love of good, which has never left my heart, turned them to purposes at once useful and potentially beneficial to morality"). In the beginning of what became *La Nouvelle Héloïse*, Rousseau's blond and weak heroine, Julie, engaged in a premarital affair with her tutor. Rousseau says that a weak girl is an object of pity who may find some appeal in love/sex, and who is often no less lovable because of her weakness. Rousseau says that there is nothing more revolting than the pride of an adulterous woman who explicitly tramples her duties underfoot and expects her husband to be grateful when she sees that he ignores her adulterous ways. Rousseau says:

> Les êtres parfaits ne sont pas dans la nature, et leurs leçons ne sont pas assez près de nous. Mais qu'une jeune personne, née avec un cœur aussi tender qu'honnête, se laisse vaincre à l'amour étant fille, et retrouve, étant femme, des forces pour le vaincre à son tour, et redevenir vertueuse, quiconque vous dira que ce tableau dans sa totalité est scandaleux et n'est pas utile est un menteur et un hypocrite; ne l'écoutez pas.[33]
>
> There are no perfect beings to be found in nature, and their examples are not sufficiently present to us. But that a young person, born with a heart both tender and honest, should allow herself to be conquered by love/sex before marriage, and should gather sufficient strength, when a wife, to turn the tables and regain her virtue, whoever tells you that this picture is on the whole scandalous and serve no useful purpose, is a liar and a hypocrite. Do not listen to him."

In addition to morality and marital fidelity, which Rousseau considered to be the root of all social order, he says he had another objective in mind when he decided to make *La Nouvelle Héloïse* into a novel, that "de concorde et de paix publique"[34] ("of harmony and the public peace"). Rousseau made the two characters of Wolmar and Julie (the married couple in the latter part of the novel) with an enthusiasm that led him to hope that he had made them both "amiables" ("likeable"), and what is more, "l'un par l'autre"[35] ("one because of the other").

In response to contemporary interpreters who see something "feminst-friendly" in Julie, I will clarify a few key points. Recall that for Rousseau, power in relationships "consists in the capacity to produce effects ... changes in the life, attitudes, and behaviour [sic] of the possessor of power and of those upon whom he [or she] exerts his [or her] power."[36] Schwartz is correct on this point: it is *only* in the sexual relationship, and with her sexual charms within marriage that woman's power should be exercised. Handling the household accounts, taking care of domestic issues throughout the community, these are some of the *duties* of a virtuous wife, and these are acts performed by Julie. We know that Julie has sexual passion for her former tutor/lover, and that she has affection and respect for her husband. We know that Julie engaged in sexual intercourse prior to marriage, and apparently with her husband after marriage (they have two sons). Beyond this, we know nothing about Julie's "power" in the marital relationship. No mention is made at all regarding the sexual relations between Julie and Wolmar, her husband, so we do not know if they engage in the simulated rape described in Chapter I of this project and Book V of *Émile*. We know that Julie is *dutiful*.

Julie is held in high esteem by all who know her, but she does not employ her sexual charms – she does not flirt, and although she makes requests, there is no acquiescence on the part of others. There is no equality between the sexes, but Julie does possess metaphysical and moral liberty. Julie herself says "Je suis femme et mère, je sais me tenir à mon rang"[37] ("I am a woman and a mother, I know how to keep my place"). Julie is always aware that she is being judged by others, that she is dependent upon the judgments and opinions not only of her husband, but of all others. Moreover, Julie internalizes those judgments. Thus, with regard to possessing individual liberty in the senses of being free from *internal* constraints, Julie is not free. Julie freely entered into a premarital affair, and she never lets anyone forget her remorse and guilt for her premarital sexual encounter. Although Julie would prefer to marry her tutor/lover, she does enter into the marriage arranged by her father of her own free will. This is the extent to which "liberty" can be understood in Julie, and she is certainly not representative of Rousseau's "ideal" of liberty.

For Rousseau, being a mother is a duty. There is no natural "maternal instinct." It is through breastfeeding that a woman will bond with her child. There is very little mention in Julie's letters of her children. Occasionally she will mention an outing, or watching them play. Indeed, the upbringing of her sons is modeled after Rousseau's own proposed domestic education for males. Julie says,

> Je nourris des enfants et n'ai pas la presumption de vouloir former des hommes. J'espère ... que de plus dignes mains se chargeront de ce nogle employ ... la function don't je suis chargée n'est pas d'élever mes fils, mais de les

preparer pour être élevés . Jen e fais même en cela que suivre de point en point les système de M. de Wolmar; et plus j'avance, plus j'éprouve combine il est excellent et juste, et combine il s'accorde avec le mien . . . Les seules lois qu'on leur impose auprès de nous sont celles de la liberté meme, savoir, de ne pas plus géner la compagnie qu'elle ne les gene, de ne pas crier plus haut qu'on ne parle; et comme on ne les oblige point de s'occuper de nous, je ne veux pas non plus qu'ils prétendent nous occuper d'eux.[38]

I nurture children and do not presume to try to form men. I hope . . . that worthier hands will take on this noble task . . . the role I am entrusted with is not to raise my sons, but to prepare them to be educated. Even in that I am doing no more than following Monsieur de Wolmar's system point by point, and the further I go, the more I realize how excellent and just it is, and how well it accords with mine . . . The only laws we impose on them [her sons] in our company are those of freedom itself, namely, that they not bother company more than it bothers them, that they not shout louder than one speaks, and as we do not oblige them to concern themselves with us, neither do I wish them to pretend to occupy us with/about them.

The objective, of course, is to prevent her sons from becoming dependent upon her, or anyone else. There is not a great deal in Julie's account of her interactions with her sons that suggests a "maternal image" in anyone's view except perhaps that of Rousseau. In relating this novel to *Émile*, Rousseau points out the natural religion in *Émile* that was a challenge to religious institutions had previously appeared in *La Nouvelle Héloïse* without criticism. Rousseau says that *Du contrat social* is related to his *Discours sur les fondements de l'inégalité parmi les hommes*, in that all that was challenging in the former had previously appeared in the latter.[39]

CONCLUDING REMARKS

With regard to consistency, Rousseau's sexual politics *is* consistent with his objectives of restoring the family and restoring virtue. By socializing women to be virtuous, to be concerned with how their actions are interpreted by others, to love their duties and to want to be mothers – and to engage in sexual intercourse with their husbands and no other men – this is where woman fits in Rousseau's philosophical project. Without virtuous women, there will be no virtuous men, and there will be no solid family structure. Unless women's power and sphere of activity are restricted, men will be subject to the opinions and judgments of women (i.e., guided by *amour-propre*).

Rousseau's sexual politics is consistent with, even essential to, his philosophical project. Moreover, Rousseau's sexual politics and his philosophical project reinforce the interpersonal and institutional oppression of women.

It should also be clear that attempts to derive a feminist-friendly reading of Rousseau's views on women are unwarranted. In the next Chapter, I will illuminate additional consequences for women of Rousseau's sexual politics, namely, the self-estrangement/alienation of women, *being* psychologically oppressed, and *living* in bad fait.

NOTES

1. In this project I explicate the views of Nicole Fermon, Joel Schwartz, Penny A. Weiss, and Carole Pateman. All four of these interpreters offer a different account of Rousseau's philosophical orientation, his definitive philosophical project, how his various works are related to that project – and *which* works are relevant, and all offer a conclusion as to whether or not Rousseau's sexual politics is consistent with, or contradictory to, his philosophical project.

2. Fermon, Nicole. *Domesticating Passions: Rousseau, Woman, and Nation.* Hanover: Weselyan University Press, 1997, p. 4.

3. Ibid., p. 3.

4. Ibid., p. 11.

5. Ibid., p. 175.

6. Ibid.

7. Schwartz, Joel. *The Sexual Politics of jean-Jacques Rousseau.* Chicago: The University of Chicago Press, 1984, p. 151.

8. Ibid., p. 144.

9. Weiss, Penny A. *Gendered Community: Rousseau, Sex, and Politics.* New York: New York University Press, 1991, p. 90.

10. Ibid., p. 129.

11. Ibid., p. 232.

12. Ibid., p. 9.

13. Pateman, Carole. *The Disorder of Women: Democracy, Feminism, and Political Thought.* Stanford: Stanford University Press, 1989, p. 6.

14. Pateman, Carole. *The Sexual Contract.* Stanford: Stanford University Press, 1988, p. 232.

15. Pateman also claims that not only do Rousseau's contracts deny liberty to women, they fail to preservie liberty for men. Rousseau does not restore absolute liberty to men, but his sexual politics and his philosophical project do maximize liberty for men. Moreover, in Chapter I, I showed that Rousseau does preserve metaphysical liberty for women, and the civil liberties women were granted in his time. Rousseau makes moral liberty a possibility for women, and he restricts women's liberty to come and go as they please, to choose projects outside of their domestic sphere and duties. Rousseau denies psychological liberty (the most important liberty) to women.

16. Rousseau, Jean-Jacques. *Émile ou De l'éducation.* Paris: Gallimard, 1969, p. 79.

17. Ibid.

18. See Vera Lee. *The Reign of Women in Eighteenth-Century France*, Cambridge: Schenkman Publishing Company, pp. 19-27. Rousseau does not distinguish between the aristocracy and the *haute bourgeoisie*. According to Lee, the *haute bourgeoisie* "considered themselves noble and bore aristocratic names because their families or husbands had recently (that is, within the previous hundred years or so) been lucky enough to obtain titles of liberty" (p. 16). The aristocracy, on the other hand, possessed inherited titles, and could trace their nobility back at least four hundred years.

19. Rousseau, Jean-Jacques. *Les Confessions*. Paris: Gallimard, 1959, p. 431

20. Rousseau, Jean-Jacques. *Discours sur les sciences et les arts*. Paris: Gallimard, 1964, p. 45.

21. Rousseau, Jean-Jacques. *Discours sur l'origine et les fondements de l'inégalité parmi les hommes*. Paris: Gallimard, 1969, p. 98.

22. Ibid.

23. Rousseau, Jean-Jacques. *Lettre à d'Alembert*. Paris: Garnier-Flammarion, 1967, p. 166.

24. Rousseau, *Émile*, p. 539.

25. Rousseau, *Lettre*, p. 167.

26. Ibid., p. 209.

27. Ibid., 113.

28. Rousseau, *Les Confessions*, p. 491.

29. Ibid., p. 616.

30. Ibid., p. 520.

31. Ibid., p. 524.

32. Ibid., p. 525.

33. Ibid.

34. Ibid.

35. Ibid., p. 527.

36. Dent, N. J. H. *A Rousseau Dictionary*. Cambridge: Blackwell Publishers, 1992, p. 195.

37. Rousseau, Jean-Jacques. *La Nouvelle Heloïse*. Paris: Garnier-Flammarion, 1967, p. 437.

38. Ibid.

39. Rousseau, *Les Confessions*, 493.

Chapter III

Rousseau and the Nineteenth Century Novel of Female Adultery: Alienation, Psychological Oppression, and Bad Faith in Rousseau and Flaubert

INTRODUCTION

In Chapter I, I explicated Jean-Jacques Rousseau's identity politics, his sexual politics, and key elements of his proposed domestic education for women (i.e., the socialization of women). Woman, in the civil state, according to Rousseau, possesses the human characteristics of *perfectibilité* and metaphysical liberty (free will). Recall that *perfectibilité* is the faculty that allows women (and men) to learn to be what they *must* be in society. Rousseau's account of what women *must* be in society is consistent with common beliefs and supported by laws in his time (and into the twentieth century). Of the three natural action-guiding passions possessed by man (i.e., humans), woman, in Rousseau, possesses only one–*l'amour*, the passion that makes one sex necessary to the other. Woman, in Rousseau does not possess the natural action-guiding passion of *pitié*. This is the passion that takes man outside himself; it joins man the individual with society. In denying woman this passion, Rousseau removes even the desire for social interactions outside the domestic sphere. The third action-guiding passion, *amour de soi* (self-preservation) is a self-focused love, unaware of others. Through *pitié*, the individual becomes aware of others. *Amour de soi* is tempered by *pitié*, which takes one outside of oneself and allows one to find ones' footing with others in the moral order. In denying woman *pitié*, Rousseau is not attributing to her *amour de soi*. Instead, Rousseau makes an artificial action-guiding passion, *amour-propre*, one of woman's governing principles.

David Gauthier explains that

> ... *amour de soi* is linked to our sentiment of existence. As long as it alone holds sway, each person unreflectively senses his existence in himself. But as it comes

> to be transformed into *amour propre*, each senses his existence not in himself, but in his relation to those whom he perceives as other. It is the regard that others have for me, their concern with my power, or their contempt for my lack of power, their valuing or disdaining my assistance, their fearing or ignoring my opposition, that form the basis of my own self-conception. I am no longer psychologically self-sufficient, and so no longer free; I seek the recognition of the other that confers prestige . . . [1]

Gauthier adds that depending on the opinions of others for one's sentiment (awareness) of existence "is to be alienated from oneself."[2] In making woman dependent upon the opinions of men (until a man recognizes her, she is nothing), Rousseau denies her individual liberty (psychological independence). This dependence on the opinions and judgments of others for one's sentiment of existence, the denial of psychological liberty as well as economic, material and physical liberty leaves woman not only socially alienated, but psychologically alienated. This is what women were taught long before Rousseau and long after (into the twentieth century, still today).

My interest is woman's *psychological* alienation. My objective is to examine, through literature, what happens, at the individual level, to a woman's psyche when she is self-estranged, when she internalizes the opinions and judgments of others concerning not only her actions but her degree of humanness, her purpose, her place, her value–her identity. What happens when woman is psychologically dependent upon others? This psychological alienation results in women *being* psychologically oppressed, and *living* in bad faith (or living inauthentically).

I will begin with a brief description of psychological oppression and bad faith. This will not be an in-depth analysis of these concepts, but is intended to provide a general idea of the issues to focus on in the literary works. I will examine psychological oppression and bad faith in two novels of female adultery: Rousseau's unfinished sequel to *Émile, Les Solitaires*, and Gustave Flaubert's novel, *Madame Bovary*. I will provide an overview of the importance of the novel of female adultery (as explained by Bill Overton) in understanding the implications of making women dependent upon the opinions of others. Finally, I will turn to the literary works of Rousseau and Flaubert to illustrate how woman's self-estrangement, or alienation, results in psychological oppression and bad faith. Rousseau was influential in the writings of Flaubert whose novel, *Madame Bovary*, is a social commentary on the status of women in the nineteenth century–very much the same as in Rousseau's time. The morality or immorality of adultery is not my concern. I am interested in the psychological dependence of women on men and how this affects their actions. The morality or immorality of adultery is not my concern. I am interested in the psychological dependence of women on men and how this affects their actions.

PSYCHOLOGICAL OPPRESSION

Psychological oppression is the least understood form of oppression, and the most readily dismissed. This type of oppression concerns the deep-seated beliefs of the individual, which are not easily detectable, even to the individual herself. When these beliefs surface and are recognized, a common remedy suggested for the psychologically oppressed is "just stop believing that," whatever *that* might be. Women are not born psychologically oppressed any more than they are born 'woman' as defined by society other individuals, and ultimately, themselves. For Rousseau, 'power' in relations with others means the ability to influence, or produce effects in the life, beliefs, and behavior of the possessor of power, and the one over whom power is exerted. These can be one and the same individual. Externally, the power over woman's life, attitudes, beliefs, and behavior consists of laws, religious doctrine, ideology, and individual men over individual women (as well as individual women over other women). Internally, when one is psychologically oppressed, the possessor of power over one's life, attitudes, and behavior is the individual herself.

Sandra Lee Bartky explains that to be psychologically oppressed

> ... is to be weighed down in your mind; it is to have a harsh dominion exercised over your self-esteem. *The psychologically oppressed become their own oppressor*; they come to exercise harsh dominion over their own self-esteem. Differently put, psychological oppression can be regarded as the 'internalization of intimations of inferiority.'[3]

Psychological oppression is often confused with depression. If we look at synonyms for 'depression' and 'oppression,' the difference becomes evident. Synonyms for 'depression' include (feelings)'despair', 'hopelessness', 'desolation,' and 'despondency.' Synonyms for 'oppression' include (external): 'domination', 'coercion', 'tyranny,' 'cruelty', 'repression', 'suppression', 'power', and 'control.' Being *oppressed* can, and does, result in being *depressed*, and it is from a state of depression that one will act (or not). To be *psychologically* oppressed is to exert domination, tyranny, cruelty, repression, suppression . . . over *oneself*. Because one *believes* one is inferior, for example, one will *act* inferior.

Bartky says that two ways in which psychological oppression can occur are when an individual internalizes stereotypes about oneself and the belief that one is a sexual object (i.e., stereotyping and sexual objectification–both in Rousseau). Present in both forms of psychological oppression is what Bartky refers to as 'fragmentation,' defined as:

> ... the splitting of the whole person into parts of a person which, in stereotyping, may take the form of a war between a 'true' and 'false' self–or, in sexual objectification, the form of an often coerced and degrading identification of a person with her body.[4]

This fragmenting of oneself, this war between one's 'true' and 'false' self, can be understood as what occurs when one attempts to live in accordance with the stereotype of woman (e.g., "all women are maternal,"), when in actuality, this is not what one is at all. One publicly *pretends* to conform to the stereotype, but struggles internally, suppressing what one knows to be true about oneself. Fragmentation through sexual objectification can occur when one internalizes negative beliefs about women's bodies, being perceived as a sexual object rather than an individual, experiencing a sense of shame because the female body is degraded, or trying not to look feminine, belief that one's body is inferior or a source of shame. This can also occur when a woman believes that it is through the use of her body, her sexual charms, that she has power, and that she can attain liberty. An awareness of negative attitudes about women's sexuality can result in a sense of shame if a woman experiences sexual desires.

Ann E. Cudd adds to Bartky's account of psychological oppression by explaining how psychological oppression indirectly harms the individual. Cudd says:

> Indirect psychological harms occur when the beliefs and values of the privileged or oppressor groups are subconsciously accepted by the subordinate and assimilated into their self-concept or value/belief scheme. Indirect forces thus work through the psychology of the oppressed while benefiting the privileged.[5]

This is how stereotyping and/or sexual objectification *by others* seeps into one's psyche. The origin of oppressive beliefs is external. This is reflected in Rousseau in his proposal that females be taught the ideology of his day. Women must first *believe* they are 'woman,' then they will *become* 'woman'–conforming to the stereotypical view of women as sexual objects. Cudd also explains three internal forces that harm the oppressed–how one harms oneself:

> The first is that of shame and low self-esteem, which are the emotive and cognitive forces involved in seeing oneself as of less worth than others. The second is the cognitive process of false consciousness, which is a cognitive process of

coming to believe in an ideology that oppresses oneself. The third is deformed desire, which is the combined affective and cognitive process of value formation, in which the oppressed come to desire that which is oppressive.[6]

This first force of harm is related to one's "sentiment of existence," awareness or perception of oneself as a being of less worth than others. Cudd's second harmful force, the *process* of internalization (an act of the mind) is how one comes to *believe* in the 'false' self presented by ideology. This process for Rousseau must begin in childhood, before a female has been exposed to other views on women. The third harmful force, deformed desire, is also evident in Rousseau. If women understand the utility of their subordination, and that they are valued as wives and mothers, that they will be respected, they will *desire* the status of motherhood and their social alienation. Women will *desire* the abdication of liberty.

Cudd says that these forces of harm are *"self-inflicted wounds*, but wounds that have been inflicted with the weapon that society provides the oppressed."[7] The explanations of psychological oppression in Bartky and Cudd illuminate the relationship between the individual and society, between psychological oppression and institutional oppression, as well as interpersonal oppression. The relationship between institutional oppression, interpersonal oppression, and psychological oppression, is a vicious cycle. These levels of oppression are mutually reinforcing; where one exists, all three will exist. Psychological oppression is more than a problem for individuals. It is a social/political issue as well. In this chapter, my interest is the relationship between women in marriage–the interpersonal–and women as individual agents–the psychological.

The language of psychological oppression is harsh: 'weighed down', 'self-inflicted wounds', 'deformed desire'. Rousseau is just as direct and harsh in his account of adulterous women as 'vile' and 'foul.' It is important to pay heed to these harsh terms–they reveal attitudes, ideologies, and they convey a message that is then internalized, resulting in psychological oppression.

BAD FAITH

To *be* psychologically oppressed is to *live* in bad faith, or to live inauthentically. Understanding bad faith will provide insight into exactly *how* women act as their own oppressors as well as illuminate 'fragmentation.' Bad faith, understood as roughly synonymous with 'self-deception' refers to a mode of living involving three types of conduct. Hazel E. Barnes simplifies the complex notion of bad faith in the existential thought of Simone de Beauvoir (which she appropriates from Jean-Paul Sartre).[8] Barnes explains that bad faith always involves a shift between two meanings of the verb '*être*' (to be): Being-in-itself, and Being-for-itself. It might be helpful in discussing humans to think of this as Being-in-myself and Being-for-myself.

Being-*in*-itself refers to the *fact* of one's existence–"I am." Recall in Rousseau that the little girl with her doll is *nothing* until a man sees her, and for the eighteenth-century aristocratic female, it was only in marriage that she could *become someone*. This is "facticity," existing as an actual, finite object in the world, occupying a definite place in time and space. This mode of Being concerns the past and the present. Being-*for*-itself (or myself) refers to "becoming," transcendence, *choosing to make of oneself what one will*, or in Rousseau's language, *perfectibilité* and metaphysical liberty (we are free to *choose* who and what we will become). This sense of Being concerns the present (this moment) and the future.

The relationship between psychological oppression and bad faith is brought to light in the modes of *living* in bad faith. Bad faith involves a metaphysical play on words. That is, simultaneously using the two meanings of "Being" in a way that is advantageous. The advantage may be such that it reinforces or encourages restraints on one's individual (as well as civil) liberty, or, as Cudd explains, desiring that which oppresses. In *Le deuxième sexe*, Beauvoir says:

> Refuser d'être l'Autre, refuser la complicité avec l'homme, ce serait pour elles renoncer à tous les avantages que l'alliance avec la caste supérieure peut leur conférer. L'homme-suzerain protégera matéiellement la femme-lige et il se chargera de justifier son existence: avec le risqué economic esquive le risqué métaphysique d'un liberté qui doit inventer ses fins sans secours.[9]
>
> To refuse to be the Other, to refuse the complicity with man, this would be for them [women] to renounce all of the advantages which the alliance with the superior caste can confer to them. Man-suzerain [feudal lord] will materially protect woman-lige [vassal] and will make it his business to justify her existence: with the economic risk comes the metaphysical risk of a liberty which must invent her ends without assistance.

Historically, and still today, it has been advantageous, economically, for women to accept their subordinate status in society. That is, there were reasons for women (especially married women) to acquiesce. On 13 July 1965, after Beauvoir wrote and published *Le deuxième sexe*, a French law was passed that preserved "the husband's title as head of the family, granted women the right to employment without their husband's consent, and also the right to administer their property as they saw fit."[10] On 4 June 1970, another French law "adopted the principle of shared spousal responsibility in the family."[11] The domestic education (socialization) of females in twentieth century, as explained in *Le deuxième sexe*, mirrors that of the eighteenth and nineteenth century woman. Rousseau appropriated the ideology of his time, which was in place in the nineteenth century. Women in all three centuries were taught to be dependent upon a man for economic security. Women were defined in terms of their dependence upon men. Marriage was still considered to be the best option for women, the preferred choice. Women, in Beauvoir's time (and still today) *believed* they were economically, materially, intellectually, morally, and psychologically dependent upon a man–and they were taught to be so dependent.

Justifying woman's existence, her "Being-in-itself," is to influence woman's "sentiment of existence." Women risk the loss of identity in rejecting the way in which women have been defined. This risk to metaphysical liberty brings into question who and what "I am," one's 'facticity.' Woman must then choose to be what she wants to be, without assistance–with no economic security, and no clear sense of self, or identity.

Beauvoir maintains that the renunciation of liberty allows women to avoid taking responsibility for their own lives and their own identity. A woman need not ask *"what do I exist as?"* or *"who am I?"* Nor does a woman need to ask *"what, or who, will I become?"* These are not easy questions to answer. These are questions of the utmost importance: it is one's *life* that is at issue. Beauvoir is addressing adult women, not the child who is yet to be influenced by societal beliefs and attitudes. Having been raised to be dependent, being on one's own, responsible for oneself, can be frightening.

The second type of bad faith conduct involves a pursuit of sincerity, which is actually *in*sincerity.[12] Sincerity is "the determination to be for oneself and for others whatever [and whoever] one actually is,"[13] as opposed to living as a fragmented self, attempting to conform to stereotypes or the way in which one has been defined by others, or not relying on the opinions of others for one's "sentiment of existence." The distinction between *what* one is and *who* one is needs to be preserved. Recall from Chapter I that for Rousseau (before and into present) *what* woman is, a different kind of being, animal, sex (her body), determines what she *must* be in the marital relationship and in society. *Who* woman is, her sense of self, is then determined by *what* she is.

All of the elements of psychological oppression and bad faith mentioned here will be evident in the literary works discussed in this Chapter. Fragmentation is a key theme in the novel, *Madame Bovary*. Bill Overton provides an analysis of the importance of the novel of female adultery that will be useful in thinking about the psychological state of Rousseau's heroine Sophie and Flaubert's heroine Emma.

THE NOVEL OF FEMALE ADULTERY

In *The Novel of Female Adultery: Love and Gender in Continental European Fiction, 1830-1900*, Bill Overton says that "the novel of adultery is in effect the novel of *female* adultery."[14] Overton explains that while there are nineteenth century novels in which husbands commit adultery, those novels in which adultery is the central theme predominantly concern adultery committed by women. According to Overton, the novel of *female* adultery, as a *tradition*, "was born in France in the 1830s,"[15] and "after 1857 . . . became established in its classic form with Flaubert's *Madame Bovary*."[16]

Overton explains that what is specific to the novel of female adultery, what distinguishes this type of work from other works in which adultery occurs but is *not* the central theme, is that:

> Self-evidently, the dominant ideas of the period about marriage are crucial to this kind of fiction, especially through their consequences for the role of the wife. What defines the novel of female adultery, however, is not simply the fact that its action hinges on the wife's betrayal of wedlock, but, above all, that it displays a specific set of attitudes towards such conduct and indeed towards women in general.[17]

The attitudes towards women in Flaubert's time were still the attitudes towards women in Rousseau's time (and in Rousseau). The novel of female adultery raises questions not only concerning marriage and adultery, but also questions about female sexuality, woman's sexual objectification, man's psychological power over woman, and laws that granted husbands the right to determine the appropriate punishment for the adulterous wife. These types of novels raise questions concerning women's individual liberty, which is intimately linked to the idea that women's power in relationships with men is entirely sexual.

In Rousseau's time, adultery among the upper classes was commonplace and, for the most part, widely accepted. For Rousseau, the adulterous woman is the root cause of all social disorders and crimes. According to Rousseau, the only differences between adulterous women and prostitutes are class and marital status–which the adulterous woman loses. The adulterous woman has no place in "proper" society. As I have stated, Rousseau merely adopts the attitudes and beliefs of his time. Adultery is, for Rousseau, *the* most important issue with regard to women.

But, one might ask, why adultery? In eighteenth and nineteenth century France, women of the middle and upper classes had little, if any, choice with regard to whether or not they *would* marry, and *whom* they would marry. Laws granted husbands economic control of women, as well as control of women's bodies. Legally, she was his to do with as he pleased. While husbands could prevent women from attaining any level of economic independence, they could not always prevent women from committing adultery. Adultery as depicted in the following works is not an act of liberty, but an act of bad faith–a bad faith choice in response to a woman's situation and condition of psychological oppression. An examination of such a banal topic will, it is hoped, generate questions about the commonplace, what we claim is "just the way things are," and open our eyes to a pervasive problem for women.

ROUSSEAU'S ADULTEROUS WOMAN: SOPHIE

Sophie has been raised in the spirit of Rousseau's proposed domestic education for women. I will briefly recap some highlights of Sophie's education from Chapter I. Sophie knows that her *violence*, her power, is through sexual intercourse. Sophie knows that *all* instances of sexual intercourse are *simulated* rape, and that it is her duty to orchestrate and permit this act. Sophie has learned that women are not *really* raped, nor are they ever *really* seduced. *She* controls when and/or if sexual intercourse will occur. This is a commonly held belief today, and it is especially important in *Madame Bovary*, wherein Emma believes that through sexual intercourse she can attain some degree of individual liberty. Sophie has been taught that she possesses natural, and God-given, sexual modesty and shame to control her unlimited sexual desires. From childhood, Sophie is taught to cultivate her sexual charms–she has learned the art of getting herself looked at, and she knows that she is *nothing* until a man sees her and judges her as pretty, worthy of his esteem, and of value. Sophie has been conditioned (educated) for that one moment when he *sees* her and she *becomes* something, when she *becomes someone*. Sophie's awareness of her existence will be determined by a man. Moreover, Sophie's upbringing has conditioned her to Be-for-Others–to live in insincerity, inauthentically, in bad faith.

Sophie is also taught that, as a woman, she is "fait pour obéir à un être aussi imparfait que l'homme, souvent si plein de vices, et toujours si plein de défauts, elle doit apprendre de bonne heure à souffrir meme l'injustice, et à supporter les torts d'un mari sans se plaindre"[18] ("made to obey a being as imperfect as man, often so full of vices, and always full of defects [faults], she must learn early to suffer [endure] this very injustice, and to tolerate the wrongs of a husband without complaint"). Woman, including Sophie, is always subject to the judgment of men and public opinion. As Gauthier maintains, she is alienated, or self-estranged. Moreover, she is conditioned to live a life of bad faith, insincerity–man will take charge of her metaphysical existence. In addition to social status and economic dependence, Sophie knows that it is her duty to endure injustices such as *his* judgment, *his* indifference, and even his *adultery*.

Everything in woman's education, and in Sophie's, is designed to create a sexual object of woman *for one man* (her husband), and through him, *for society and the state.* According to Rousseau, adultery would cease to be a problem *if and only if* females are taught to control their sexual desires and focus their sexual power, influence, on their husbands. As a result of a happy home life and satisfying sex (not too frequent–he might get bored), society's other great evil–the prostitute–would cease to be a problem. Thus, it seems that for Rousseau, the virtuous woman has the added duty of ridding society of prostitutes. Man's happy sex life at home would result in no more business for prostitutes.

What Sophie is *not* taught, and what is not included in Rousseau's theoretical account of woman's proper domestic education, is how to deal with death. Following the deaths of her parents and infant daughter, Sophie is so distraught that Emile decides to take her to Paris as a distraction, and to restore to himself his agreeable and pleasing wife. This proves to be the downfall of the "ideal" family. Emile is corrupted by the "fast and loose" life of the big city, dishonoring his marriage vows by vacillating in his love and devotion for Sophie. There is a clear suggestion in *Les Solitaires* that Emile commits adultery. Emile, writing to his former tutor, says that he was drawn into the city life, "j'errois avec inquietude d'un plaisir à l'autre; je recherchois tout et j'm'ennuyois de tout; je ne me plaissois qu'où je n'étois pas, et m'étourdissois pour m'amuser"[19] ("I wandered worriedly from one pleasure to another; I looked for [sought after] everything and got bored with everything; I was only happy [there/any place] where I was not, and I ran myself dizzy to amuse myself"). This is of little consequence. Recall from Chapter I that Rousseau admits that an unfaithful husband is an unjust and cruel man. This is not, however, a *crime*, and she must endure this injustice–it is her wifely duty.

Sophie, "whose whole life has been made to revolve around love, whose entire self-esteem depends on whether she is pleasing to men,"[20] to suffer his injustices, is still ill-equipped to deal with Emile's rejection and indifference. Sophie makes a bad faith choice–she commits adultery and finds herself pregnant with another man's child. Remember, Sophie's sentiment of her own existence is dependent upon a man. She is *nothing* until a man *sees* her. Flitting around all over Paris does not leave Emile time to *see* Sophie. Sophie *knows* the consequences of her act–loss of social status, economic security, his esteem, social censure–and she will believe herself deserving of these consequences. Sophie will become her own oppressor.

Emile is convinced that Sophie is remorseful (shamed), and he admires her honesty in confessing her transgression. He *thinks* her heart has remained pure. Moreover, Emile admits that the temptations confronting Sophie in the city were more than even *he* could resist. And, well, he *did* ignore his husbandly duties! However, in the end, Emile sees no alternative but to leave

Sophie and abandon their son. Her adultery (not his) is the cause of the dissolution of the family. Whether or not *she* could remain with an adulterous husband is not an issue. According to Rousseau, it is *her duty* to preserve the family relationship.

Susan Moller Okin says that Sophie would not have been able to accept Emile's pardon even if he had offered it. For Rousseau, a woman should carry her shame with her throughout her life (as does his other literary heroine, Julie, in *La Nouvelle Héloïse*). This shame, Okin explains, would be more than Sophie could bear. Wifely adultery was considered a treasonous crime in Rousseau's day (and long afterward). The punishment for this crime could be determined by the State, the Church, or the betrayed husband. Emile is not only Sophie's husband, he is her judge: "Par la loi meme de la nature les femmes . . . sont à la merci des jugemens des hommes"[21] ("By the very law of nature women . . . are at the mercy of the judgments of men"). Man is not at the mercy of woman's judgment of his conduct.

In Emile's eyes, and he is certain this is the case for Sophie as well, she "has fallen from the pedestal of the Madonna to the gutter of the prostitute."[22] In his theoretical treatise on woman in Book V of *Émile*, woman is "naturally" sexual, and she must always fight *this* part of her being. Rousseau says that women's "honneur n'est pas seulement dans leur conduite mas dans leur reputation, et il n'est pas possible que celle qui consent à passer pour infâme puisse jamais être honnête"[23] ("honor is not soley in their conduct but in their reputation, and it is not possible that she who consents to be thought of (judged) as infamous (vile, foul) can ever be respectable"). Women must *believe* this. Here we see fragmentation, a conflict between woman's 'true' self–a naturally sexual being–and her 'false' self, the Madonna who gives the appearance of virtue, trying and failing to be what she *must* be, yet unable to deny, for Rousseau (at least what women must believe) what she is. Emile concludes that although Sophie may be remorseful, and still pure of heart, there is no guarantee that, having succumbed once, she will not succumb again. It may prove impossible for Sophie's "natural" sexuality to be controlled. Without her chaste reputation, Sophie (indeed, women in general), has no virtue left to preserve.

Emile has been educated to think for himself, *not* to be governed by public opinion. However, in this case, and in agreement with Rousseau's own position, he thinks public opinion is right. Public opinion, and the position of the state, held that a wife's adultery was a crime against her husband's honor. Emile's rationale is that this type of crime *is*, in a sense, the fault of the betrayed husband–either he made a bad choice in a wife (her *appearance* of virtue was 'false,' hiding her 'true' self) or he governs her badly. Nonetheless, Emile cannot forgive Sophie. Sophie's seducer is not to blame, of course. As we know, according to Rousseau, she could have refrained if she had really wanted to. Sexual intercourse is *woman's* domain, she decides when and/or if sexual intercourse occurs. Sophie's act of adultery was an act of free will, she *chose* to commit adultery.

Rousseau does not provide the reader with Sophie's point of view, or her reasons for committing adultery. However, we do know that Sophie was conditioned from birth to be docile, timid, economically, materially, and psychologically dependent, subjugated, relying on her sexual charms to get a husband, and to *accept his judgment without complaint*. Emile's indifference would be intolerable for a woman like Sophie. In his indifference, he did not *see* her, and he did not *desire* her (he sought other pleasures)–she was not a doll to be admired, *she was nothing*. With no other options than marriage, Sophie's (and woman's) domain is so limited that, whether by necessity or choice, she is incapable of surviving in the world on her own. According to literary tradition, Sophie is left with two options: prostitution or death. In the "real" world, Sophie might have retired to a convent. Either way, symbolically or physically, it is the end for Sophie. We do not know Sophie's reaction to her situation. We do know that she is Rousseau's creation, and she believes everything about herself that Rousseau claims women *must* believe–that she is vile, foul, and deserving of her punishment. Sophie's dependence on man to provide justification of her existence resulted in a bad faith choice, and she knew what the consequences would be. This is the result of making woman dependent upon man for her "sentiment of existence."

FLAUBERT'S MADAME BOVARY AND EMMA[24]

Critics of *Madame Bovary,* and the protagonist Emma, question whether Emma was wrong to be so disappointed in her fate (marriage and motherhood). What do we know about Emma, and how does she come to commit adultery? Like Sophie, Emma is not a beauty, but she does know the art of getting looked at. According to Rousseau, this must be a lesson all females learn. Charles Bovary's (Emma's future husband) first meeting with Emma reveals a very sensual woman. Charles is aware of her feminine charms. He notices that "tout en cousant, elle se piquait les doigts, qu'elle portrait ensuite a sa bouche pour les sucer"[25] ("as she sewed, she pricked her fingers, which she then put in her mouth to suck them"). A very erotic image. On another visit, as was customary in the country (Emma is from the country), Emma offers Charles an alcoholic beverage. Pouring just a bit in her own glass, and after touching their glasses together, she

... le porta à sa bouche. Comme il était Presque vide, elle se renversait pour boire: et, la tête en arrière, les lèvres avancées, le cou tendu, elle riait de ne rien sentir, tandis que le bout de sa langue, passant entre ses dents fines, léchait à petits coups le fond du verre.[26]

... brought it to her mouth. As it was almost empty, she leaned back to drink: and, her head back, lips protruding, neck extended, she laughed because she tasted nothing, while the tip of her tongue passing between her small teeth, daintily licked the bottom of the glass.

Charles is very aware of Emma's sexual charms while he is in her presence. Later, away from her, he remembers her in her domestic role, performing domestic chores. Were it not for the fact that, in these initial meetings, Charles Bovary is a married man, Rousseau would be so proud of Emma's use of her charms!

In an early meeting with Charles, Emma reveals that she does not like the country, a hint that Charles misses. Emma is not going to be happy in charge of her own household. Emma reads voraciously–not only women's magazines and cheap romances that are circulated among her convent schoolmates, but also the novels of George Sand and, after she is married, Rousseau. Like other girls of her age (like Sophie), Emma fantasizes about a Byronic hero who will appear and sweep her off her feet. When opportunity presents itself in the form of Charles Bovary–an older man now widowed, and a doctor–Emma does precisely what society has conditioned her to do, marry a man whose status will raise her up on the social ladder. Emma believes, and rightly so for a rural, nineteenth-century French woman, that she has three options: the convent (which she already rejected), life on the farm (which she hates), or marriage. Emma chooses marriage, but it takes her father some time to convince her that this is a good choice.

Emma makes an attempt to be a good wife and to find happiness in her domestic status. Charles comes home every night "to a glowing fire, the table set, the furniture arranged comfortably, and a charming woman, neatly dressed," a young wife "who strives to give herself over completely to loving him."[27] Emma is trying to be the stereotypical good wife while suppressing her sensual "nature." This is a form of fragmentation.

Thus far, however, Emma *appears* to be exactly what Rousseau would approve of. She successfully used her sexual charms to get a husband. Now, she dedicates herself to making his life pleasant. Alas, although Emma does initially try (and she will try again) to be a proper wife, she soon feels suffocated. Emma keeps herself busy. She keeps the house superbly, keeps track of Charles's accounts, entertains *his* friends and their neighbors, and waits up late into the night to serve him a hot meal when he returns from seeing patients. She makes needlepoint slippers for her husband, draws pictures, and arranges fruit in the shape of a pyramid for his enjoyment. However, while Charles thinks very highly of himself because he "possédait une pareille femme"[28] ("possessed such a wife"), Emma feels caged in domestic mediocrity.

It is when Emma gives birth to her daughter that we learn what Emma wants. Emma had hoped for a son,

> ... cette idée d'avoir pour enfant un male était comme la revanche en espoir de toutes ses impuissances passes. Un homme, au moins, est libre; il peut parcourir les passions et les pays, traverser les obstacles, mordre aux bonheurs les plus lointains. Mais une femme est empêchée continuellement. Inerte et flexible à la fois, elle a contre elle les mollesses de la chair avec les dependences de la loi. Sa volonté comme le voile de son chapeau retenu par un cordon, palpate àtous les vent, il y a toujours quelque désir qui entraîne, quelque convenance qui reticent.[29]
>
> ... the idea of having a male child was an anticipatory revenge for all her earlier helplessness. A man, at least, is free. He can explore passions and countries, surmount obstacles, taste the most exotic pleasures. But a woman is continually held back. Inert and flexible at the same time, she has both the susceptibilities of the flesh and legal restrictions against her. Her will like the veil of her hat that is tied by a ribbon, reacts to every wind, there is always some desire to respond to, some convention that restricts action.

Here we are given insight into the life of a nineteenth-century woman, much like the life of an eighteenth-century woman.

Emma longs to confide her melancholy to someone. However, there is no husband who listens to her (Charles never really *hears* her), no priest (she seeks help there, only to be dismissed by the curé, who first ignores her presence, then ignores her distress). Like Sophie, Emma has no woman friend to validate her sense of suffocation, no woman to echo or debate her when she wonders, several times throughout the novel, "Pourquoi, mon Dieu, me suis-je mariée?"[30] ("Why, my God, am I married?"). Would she have had more liberty remaining under her father's roof? Would she have been happier in the convent? Emma is never content with where she is. As in Rousseau's time, class boundaries are strict, so the wet-nurse to whom Emma must entrust with her newborn child (as is appropriate for the wife of a physician) cannot be considered a friend. Emma's sole confidante is her dog. (Telling lonely people to get a pet is quite common). Still, Emma tries to find creative ways of dealing with her predicament. She continues to attempt to suppress her 'true' self, the unhappy, lonely woman. Finally, Emma *begins to acknowledge her rage.* "Forbidden the agency to *act* on her own life, Emma gradually learns patriarchy's bitter, basic lesson: a woman may define herself–advance, function, be visible, even rebel–only through men."[31] Overton relates an early scene in the novel to reveal that Emma's condition is more than mere discontent with her lot in life:

> The scene shows a man and wife at table, the most everyday situation imaginable . . . Here . . . is a picture of discomfort, and not a momentary and passing one, but a chronic discomfort, which completely rules an entire life, Emma Bovary's. To be sure, various things come later, among them the love episodes [adulterous acts]; but no one could see the scene at table as part of the exposition for a love episode, just as no one would call *Madame Bovary* a love story in general. The novel is the representation of an entire human existence which has no issue; and our passage is a part of it, which, however, contains the whole. It is a random moment from the regularly recurring hours at which the husband and wife eat together. They are not quarreling; there is no sort of tangible conflict. *Emma is in complete despair*, but her despair is not occasioned by any definite catastrophe; there is nothing purely concrete which she has lost or for which she wished. Certainly, she has many wishes, but they are entirely vague—elegance, love, a varied life . . .[32]

Overton adds that "there must have always been such unconcrete despair, but no one ever thought of taking it seriously in literary works before; such a formless tragedy . . . which is set in motion by the general situation itself,"[33] is, Overton alleges, represented for the first time by Flaubert, who presented this despair in "people of slight intellectual culture and fairly low social station; certainly he is the first who directly captures the chronic character of this psychological situation."[34] This is one way in which Flaubert is important to a discussion of the psychological oppression of women. Although psychological oppression has not been discussed in philosophy until recently, it is not a new phenomenon.

Overton relates Emma's situation of despair to that of an account of a young woman of the period "in anguished contemplation of marriage":

> 'I am not even able to live alone, being obliged to take from others, not only in order to live but also in order to be protected, since social convention does not allow me to have independence. And yet the world finds me guilty of being the only person I am at liberty to be; not having useful or productive work to do, not having a calling except marriage, and not being able to look by myself for someone who will suit me, I am full of cares and anxieties.[35]

Overton says that Emma has started from a similar position, "but lacking the ability to analyze it, she has entered into marriage . . . with the one suitor who comes forward, only to find herself still dependent, superfluous, and unsatisfied."[36] Overton says that "in such circumstances, despair is concrete enough."[37] many women can find themselves in Emma, and men can learn a great deal about women from this novel.

It is from this state of despair that Emma commits adultery. Emma actually has three lovers, and all three betray her. Emma's first adulterous affair is with Rodolphe, an aristocratic "playboy" who deliberately seduces Emma, then finds her boring–his standard conquest pattern. Critics and commentators have questioned what Emma sees in Rodolphe. She says it quite clearly: "vous êtes libre . . . riche"[38] ("you are free . . . rich"). Rodolphe can choose his projects, his life, and he is economically independent. Emma comes to associate liberty, as well as love, with wealth. Moreover, while everyone else calls her "Madame Bovary," identifying her, defining her, as wife and mother, Rodolphe calls her "Emma," which leads her to believe that he sees *her*–the 'true' Emma, an individual rather than someone's wife or someone's mother. This is an illustration of fragmentation, a component of psychological oppression.

Following their first lovemaking session, Emma experiences a certain sense of revenge. Having a lover is, for Emma, a sign that she is grown up. Moreover, taking a lover is a sign of rebellion for Emma, revolt against society's restrictions. Thus, in her own mind, Emma thinks she is free. It is still common to hear today that women's liberation is all about sexual freedom. Recall that for Rousseau, woman's *violence,* her power, is *sexual.* This is an illusory power. As Emma's illusions fall away, she feels humiliated, subjugated, and fearful of Rodolphe. Emma's constant 'do you love me?' questions begin, not because she is insatiable or insecure, but because Emma is dependent upon Rodolphe for her "sentiment of existence." Rodolphe eventually abandons Emma. She realizes that while Rodolphe looked at her and possessed her body, she has remained *unseen*. This is not referring to Emma's physical body, but to the person that she is–no one has seen the woman with hopes, dreams, and desires.

Léon, Emma's second lover, convinces Emma (and himself) that he has seen her, he *knows* her deepest thoughts and desires–at least he thinks he knows Emma. He never really looks for Emma. With, and for, Léon, Emma sinks to greater depths. All her creativity is spent on clever ways to conceal the affair, and the money she invests in maintaining the affair. Although Emma is criticized for her materialism, we see her sell treasured items and misuse funds for the sake of passion and her means to liberty. Passion means more to Emma than physical pleasure; it means being loved, which in turn means being seen. Recall that in Rousseau, until a woman is seen by a man, she is nothing. Emma needs a man to see beyond her physical body, but still, she depends on a man to define her. *Emma* exists when she is seen and loved by a man. *Madame Bovary* exists when she is the dutiful wife and mother.

Deep in debt, Emma holds firmly to what little dignity she can muster in rejecting the proposition of a lecherous notary who could save her financially–for a price, of course. Emma tells the man that she is to be pitied, but she is not for sale. Bankruptcy looms and discovery of Emma's affairs by her husband is imminent. Some of the villagers are already aware that Madame Bovary has compromised herself. Léon refuses to steal money from his employer to assist Emma. Rodolphe, having returned, refuses Emma's offer to reignite their affair in exchange for a loan–he asks Emma why he should pay for something he already had for free. This has been interpreted as an allusion to one course of action left open to Emma, and a course of action she has already rejected: prostitution. Emma's terror, a dark future with no escape, is becoming her reality. Emma is not concerned about Charles's discovery of her adulterous acts. Emma cannot bear the thought of a life without what she perceives as liberty. Emma sees death as her only remaining route to liberty, and she eagerly embraces this path. It is while she awaits death that Emma is betrayed by her third lover–Christ.

Emma's yearning for Christ[39] is a dominant theme throughout the novel. As Emma lies dying, she was "collant ses lèvres sur le corps de l'Homme-Dieu, elle y déposa de toute sa force expirante le plus grand baiser d'amour qu'elle eût jamais donné"[40] ("pressing her lips to the body of the Man-God, she placed on it, with all her waning strength the most passionate kiss of love that she had ever given"). In the convulsions of her agonizing death (Emma ate arsenic), Emma almost attains a spiritual peace–but that too is violated by the guttural song of a blind beggar outside her window. Finally, "*Elle n'existait pas*"[41] ("*She did not exist/She was no more*"). In death as in life, Emma is *unseen*. As Charles looks at his wife's lifeless body, he notes:

> Des moirés frissonnaient sur la robe de satin, blanche comme un clair de lune. *Emma disparaissait dessous*; et il lui semblait que, s'épandant au-dehors d'elle-même, elle se perdait confusément dans l'entourage des choses, dans le silence, dans la nuit, dans le vent qui passait, dans les senteurs humides qui montaient.[42]
>
> On her satin dress, white as a ray of moonlight, the watered texture shimmered. *She seemed to disappear beneath it*; and it seemed to him that, she was escaping from herself, she had blended in a confused way with the surroundings, in the silence, in the night, in the passing breeze, in the damp odors that were rising.

Emma–did she ever exist for anyone other than herself? Charles wants his wife, Madame Bovary, buried in her wedding dress. Emma never felt like herself in her role as Madame Bovary. This wife and mother was the 'false' self. In the end, however, it would appear that the battle between Emma's 'false' self and her 'true' self is won by the former. Emma will go to her grave being *seen* as Madame Bovary.

58   Chapter III

Emile loved Sophie's charms more than he loved Sophie. Charles loved someone—but it was not *Emma*, whom after their initial meetings, he has never thought of as a human being outside of her domestic role. Learning later of her affairs, Charles forgives Rodolphe. Charles dies, but Rodolphe and Léon thrive, as do Christ and the Church. Only Emma is judged harshly—and *not* ironically—though she has lived and died an outsider.

CONCLUDING REMARKS

Emma internalized the social belief that through sexual relations she can attain some degree of individual liberty. Emma believes that her act of "rebellion," her adultery, is an act of freedom. It may be an act of free will, but the constraints imposed on her with regard to pursuing goals, choosing projects, etc., are never removed. Having learned patriarchy's harsh lesson, Emma comes to desire that which oppresses her, liberty through sexual intercourse.

Sophie was not allowed to transcend her past, to *become* anything other than an adulterous woman. For Rousseau, a woman must carry her "shame" with her always. Emma sought transcendence through death, unable to ever become the person she wished to be. Physically or symbolically, the options for both women are extremely limited. Society would never accept them, and social alienation is as unbearable as indifference within an interpersonal relationship.

Looking at woman's condition today, from a top-down perspective (from the social to the interpersonal, and then to the individual), it *seems* as though we have "come a long way, baby." However, as Plato informed us, appearances are often deceiving. Adopting Beauvoir's research method (observing and listening to women in the everyday world), and Albert Camus's emphasis on the relationship between belief and action (regardless of what we say, what we *really* believe is exhibited through our actions), and looking at woman's condition from the bottom-up, starting with the individual, just how far have we come? Women, and men, still believe that, in personal relationships, women have all the power, and this power is sexual. Women, it is claimed, decide when sexual intercourse will occur. This is often perceived as something to be proud of. Women, and men, continue to believe that the man should be the head of the house, he should be in charge. Men will claim that Hugh Hefner is the greatest thing that happened to women—he provided women with a venue for expressing their sexuality, thus liberating women. His contribution to the sexual revolution is still referred to as *the* defining moment of the feminist movement in the twentieth century. Women still believe that they are subject to the judgments of men *because they are*. Although I have emphasized the problem historically, in too many ways, the world of Rousseau is *our* world.

Can alienation (self-estrangement), *psychological* oppression, and bad faith (inauthenticity) be overcome? In the next, and final Chapter, I will relate Rousseau's concepts liberty, *perfectibilité*, and *pitié* to Beauvoir's concepts of liberty and authenticity. Insofar as psychological oppression is intimately connected with interpersonal oppression and institutional oppression, eradicating one form of oppression requires the simultaneous eradication of the others. We know how to go about eliminating institutional oppression, which will impact interpersonal relationships. My emphasis in Chapter IV will remain at the individual level. I will look at Beauvoir's novelette, "*La femme rompue*," as an illustration of how an individual woman can overcome alienation, psychological oppression, and living in bad faith.

NOTES

1. Gauthier, David. *Rousseau: The Sentiment of Existence*. Cambridge: Cambridge University Press, 2006, p. 10.
2. Ibid., p. 42.
3. Bartky, Sandra Lee. *Femininity and Domination: Studies in the Phenomenology of Oppression*. New York: Routledge, 1990, p. 22, my italics.
4. Ibid., p. 23.
5. Cudd, Ann E. *Analyzing Oppression*. New York: Oxford University Press, 2006, p. 176.
6. Ibid.
7. Ibid., my italics.
8. Barnes, Hazel E. *Humanistic Existentialism: The Literature of Possibility*. Lincoln, NE: University of Nebraska Press, 1959, pp. 50-54.
9. Beauvoir, Simone de. *Le deuxène sexe, I*. Paris: Gallimard, 1949/1976, p. 21.
10. Fauré, Christine. *Democracy Without Women: Feminism and the Rise of Liberal Individualism in France*. Bloomington: Indiana University Press, 1991, p. 13.
11. Ibid.
12. Some commentators refer to this as 'Being-for-oneself' versus 'Being-for-others.' In order to avoid confusing 'Being-in' and 'Being-for' language, I will adhere to Barnes's interpretation.
13. Barnes, p. 54.
14. Ibid., my italics.
15. Ibid., p. 11.
16. Ibid., p. 96.
17. Ibid.
18. Rousseau, Jean-Jacques. *Émile ou De l'éducation*. Paris: Gallimard, 1969, pp. 546-547.

19. Rousseau, Jean-Jacques. *Émile et Sophie ou Les Solitaires*. Paris: Payot & Rivages, 1994, p. 52.

20. Okin, Susan Moller. *Women in Western Political Thought*. Princeton: Princeton University Press, 1979, p. 170.

21. Rousseau, *Émile*, p. 538.

22. Okin, p. 171.

23. Rousseau, *Émile*, p. 538.

24. This is not the title of the work and the name of the female protagonist. This novel illustrates fragmentation, Madame Bovary (wife and mother) and Emma (sexual, attempting to assert some degree of independence)–the 'false' self and the 'true' self of the protagonist, respectively.

25. Flaubert, Gustave. *Madame Bovary*. Paris: Flammarion, 1986, p. 74.

26. Ibid., p. 81.

27. Ibid.

28. Flaubert, p. 102.

29. Ibid., p. 153.

30. Ibid., p. 103.

31. Overton, p. 85, my italics.

32. Ibid.

33. Ibid.

34. Ibid.

35. Ibid.

36. Ibid.

37. Flaubert, p. 205.

38. Ibid.

39. Flaubert, p. 399.

40. Ibid., p. 401, my italics.

41. Flaubert, p. 408, my italics.

42. Ibid.

Chapter IV

Rousseau and Simone de Beauvoir: Overcoming Alienation, Psychological Oppression, and Bad Faith through Liberty

INTRODUCTION

I will begin this Chapter with an explanation of how Rousseau shares important affinities with two contemporary forms of feminism–the "difference feminism" of cultural feminism and post-structural feminism, and I will note logical problems for all three positions. However, I will show that despite the problems, we need not entirely reject Rousseau by addressing the question posed in Chapter III–can alienation (self-estrangement), psychological oppression, and bad faith be *overcome*? I will propose a philosophy of liberation for women that will integrate key elements in Rousseau and the philosophy of Simone de Beauvoir. I will explicate Simone de Beauvoir's rejection of all forms of essentialism and her account of where change must begin–with women themselves. That is, I will bring to light the root of the problem for women both historically and today, according to Beauvoir, namely, identity politics and personal reponsibility. Next, I will provide Beauvoir's account of ontological liberty, social/material liberty, and moral liberty as put forth in *Pour une morale de l'ambiguïé* along with additional material regarding bad faith. At the individual/psychological level, it is with regard to metaphysical liberty, individual liberty (understood as psychological independence, not relying on others to define oneself, independence of opinions and judgments of others for one's "sentiment of existence"), *perfectibilité,* and *pitié* (as Rousseau defines this term in the civil state) that we find something "feminist-friendly" to appropriate in Rousseau. Finally, I will use Beauvoir's novelette, "*La femme rompue*" to illustrate how a woman can overcome alienation, psychological oppression (acting as her own oppressor) and living in bad faith. My emphasis remains at the individual level.

My claim is *not* that alienation, psychological oppression, and living in bad faith can be prevented. In this Chapter, I make the more modest claim that *if* the deeply imbedded beliefs a woman has internalized about herself surface (if the unconscious becomes conscious), and *if* a woman can find the courage to accept that she has acted as her own oppressor, that she is responsible for her choices, deciding for herself who she will be (i.e., defining herself), *then*, as illustrated in Beauvoir's novelette, it is *possible* to overcome alienation, psychological oppression, and bad faith. It is not easy, and it is not a "one time" deal. Living authentically, or not, is a choice one makes every day, and the first step is the most difficult. Moreover, I will show that liberty is essential to overcoming alienation, psychological oppression, and bad faith.

ROUSSEAU AND CONTEMPORARY FEMINISM

It is claimed that, moving into the third wave of feminism, the "major theoretical debate . . . is identity politics, or 'essentialism'–providing a political definition for the concept 'woman.'"[1] This need to define woman was a dominant issue for the *philosophes* in eighteenth-century France, including Rousseau. From the question "what *is* woman?" which was, and continues to be, addressed in terms of difference (anatomical, intellectual, temperament, etc.), the question becomes "what *should* she be?" Rousseau, as I explained in Chapter I, refocused the question to ask what woman *must* be. Today, as in Rousseau's time, this latter question concerns woman's place in society, her equality and liberty (both within and outside the marital relationship), her duties, and purpose. It appears that the debate has come full circle.

Linda Alcoff says that the current status of this debate with regard to identity politics is between cultural feminism, a form of essentialism, and a poststructuralist alternative, which challenges the significance of sex difference. According to Alcoff, cultural feminists (in general) claim that the *way* men have defined women has resulted in a "distortion and devaluation of feminine characteristics."[2] Cultural feminists do not object to the notion of defining 'woman', but suggest "a more accurate feminist description and appraisal" understanding "women's passivity as her peacefulness, her sentimentality as her proclivity to nurture, her subjectiveness as her advanced self-awareness."[3] Moreover, on this view, women are to be defined "by their activities and attributes in their present culture."[4] This is reminiscent of Rousseau as explicated in Chapter I. For Rousseau, women *must* be defined by their duties and purpose in the civil state. Rousseau defines woman as passive, subjugated, dependent, and in terms of her sexual function. Moreover, in Rousseau, woman is defined in terms of her duties, purpose, and guiding passion (the sexual passion) in society. Rousseau's education, or socialization, of women emphasizes women's different intellect, temperament, character, and inclinations (action guiding passions).

Post-structuralists (in general) "reject the possibility of defining 'woman' at all."[5] The post-structualist's tactic is to deconstruct all concepts of 'woman' and "argue that both feminist and misogynist attempts to define woman are politically reactionary and ontologically mistaken."[6] In order to offer a definition or characterization of 'woman', and even to speak for women, sex difference "must be replaced by a plurality of difference where [sex] loses its position of significance."[7] For the post-structuralists, we cannot define 'woman' as *human* without denying the oppression of women. Using psychoanalysis (Lacan), grammar (Derrida), and the history of discourse (Foucault), post-structuralists "'deconstruct' our concept of the subject as having an essential identity and an authentic core that has been repressed by society. There is no essential core 'natural' to us, and so there is no repression in the humanist sense."[8] As I showed in Chapter I, Rousseau's identity politics denies full humanness to woman. For Rousseau, woman is human *only* to the extent that she shares common anatomical parts with man.

The 'essentialism' of cultural feminism appears to "create homogeneous and ahistorical ideas about what it means to be a woman," and it reinforces the sexist idea of a naturalized womanhood."[9] The post-structuralist theory "eliminates the possibility of any positive conceptions upon which to base a politics."[10] Moreover, the critique of the subject seems to "deny the idea of agents capable of making change . . . post-structuralism appears to leave nothing to struggle for and no one left to make the struggle."[11] Alcoff maintains that the concept of 'woman', with regard to identity politics, is caught between Scylla and Charybdis.

Alcoff's claim presents a false dilemma. According to Alcoff, the alternatives for feminist theory appear to be *either* cultural feminism *or* the post-structural alternative. A false dilemma portrays a situation in simplistic "either-or" terms and fails to acknowledge that other possibilities exist. For example, the writers of "The Woman Identified Woman" argue that "we [women] have internalized the male culture's definition of ourselves."[12] Frederick Engels claimed that "the formation of the family as the economic unit of society was affirmed by the overthrow of mother right, the *world historical defeat of the female sex*."[13] Thus, woman's "nature" as subordinate to man pervades both the social and the domestic realms. Catherine MacKinnon states that "women remain socially defined as women in relation to men . . . The good news is, it is not biological."[14] Monique Wittig says that "not only is there no natural group 'women' (we lesbians are living proof of it), but as individuals as well we question 'woman', which for us, as for Simone de Beauvoir . . . is only a myth."[15] Wittig adds that the "first task . . . is to always thoroughly dissociate 'women' (the class within which we fight) and 'woman', the myth."[16] As I will show subsequently, these alternate views are reflected in the thought of Beauovir. My point is that not *all* difference feminists agree with the cultural feminist's account of 'woman.' Moreover, difference feminism and post-structural feminism are only two forms of feminism. In claiming that the current debate is between *only* two forms of feminism, Alcoff discounts the important contributions to feminist theory of, for example, equality feminism, liberal feminism, and existential feminism (to name only three other forms of feminism).

Essentialism (including the essentialism of Rousseau and cultural feminism) commits the fallacy of hypostatization, or the "fallacy of misplaced concreteness." This error in reasoning assumes that woman's concrete reality is consistent with the abstract definition of 'woman.' This is a failure to distinguish between essence and existence–between an ideal and reality. In defining 'woman,' Rousseau and cultural feminists (and essentialists in general) posit an abstract idea of 'woman' and assume that woman's concrete reality should be in accordance with the idea. Defining woman as passive, dependent, subjugated, for example, assumes that women are *by their very nature* passive, dependent, and subjugated. Women *act* as passive, dependent, subjugated beings because they are *taught* to act in these ways. As I illustrated in Chapter III, and as will be evidenced later in this Chapter, women's attempts to reconcile their concrete reality as 'human' with the abstract idea of 'woman' can, and does, result in fragmentation–a key component in self-alienation, psychological oppression, and living in bad faith. Granted, the concrete reality for women in terms of laws, ideology, and opportunities has, and continues to, adhere to the abstract idea of woman's place and purpose in society. However, the concrete reality of woman's *essence*, if defined as passive, dependent, subjugated, etc., undermines the concrete reality of woman's *existence* in the world, in society, as a human who can choose to define herself, to be independent, liberated, and free.

Post-structuralism presents yet another false dilemma. In addition to ignoring other possibilities, a false dilemma fails to recognize that the two alternatives could both be true. In claiming that woman is *either* human *or* oppressed, post-structuralism overlooks, or ignores, the alternative that women (and all oppressed groups) are humans who have been, and are, oppressed by political systems, other individuals, and ultimately, by themselves. It is human beings who agree to, and adhere to, the political systems that perpetuate the oppression of some humans. It is human beings who oppress other human beings, and it is human beings who act as their own oppressors. Oppression is a *human* issue. It is not necessary to deny either alternative presented by post-structualism.

An additional problem in Rousseau, cultural feminism, and post-structuralism is that the focus is entirely on woman's place and identity in society. All three ignore the psychological implications for women that are a result of being defined by others. In the end, Rousseau's identity politics, cultural feminism, and the post-structuralist claim that acknowledging women's oppression requires denying that women are human *all* perpetuate the self-estrangement, psychological oppression, and living in bad faith of women.

BEAUVOIR'S REJECTION OF ESSENTIALISM AND WOMEN'S RESPONSIBILITY

In *Brigitte Bardot and the Lolita syndrome*, Simone de Beauvoir says that "As soon as a single myth is touched, all myths are in danger."[17] In *Le deuxième sexe*, Beauvoir does far more than "touch" the myth of Woman. She launches an all-out attack, bringing into question *all* myths concerning men, women, society, culture, and how these myths influence our perception of our situation in the world.

Beauvoir rejects all forms of essentialism, or historical myths, about the nature of woman. Beauvoir says, "ce n'est pas une mystérieuse essence qui dicte aux hommes et aux femmes le bonne ou la mauvaise fois; c'est leur situation qui les dispose plus ou moins à la recherché de la vérité"[18] ("it is not a mysterious essence which/that dictates to men and to women good or bad faith; it is their situation which/that disposes them more or less to the search for truth").

The post-structuralists deny an essential nature, but they also want to deny that we can define 'woman' as 'human' without denying the oppression of women. An important passage in *Le deuxième sexe* reveals Beauvoir's position on this issue. Beauvoir asks, "Comment dans la condition féminine peut s'accomplir un être humain?"[19] ("How is it possible within the feminine condition to realize oneself as human?"). Beauvoir is talking about 'woman' as historically defined, in terms of essential properties and as, at most, partially human. Beauvoir is not denying that woman is human. The issue is that if woman is defined as non-human, or partially human, and from her oppressed condition, she cannot *realize* her humanness, or her connectedness with humanity.

In *Le deuxième sexe*, Beauvoir advocated change with regard to defining women at the social/political level. However, by 1972, Beauvoir no longer believed that a social revolution would be enough to liberate women. In *Le Nouvel Observateur*, Beauvoir says, 'Women must take their destiny into their own hands.'[20] Beauvoir says that "Si la femme se découvre comme l'inessentiel qui jamais retourne à l'essentiel, c'est qu'elle n'opère pas elle-même ce retour . . . elles ne se posent pas authentiquement comme Sujet"[21] ("If woman discovers/finds herself as the inessential which never returns to the essential, it is that she herself does not bring about this return [to the essential] . . . they [women] do not present themselves authentically as a Subject"). Beauvoir maintains that the renunciation of liberty allows women to avoid taking responsibility for their own lives and their own identity. This is the mode of bad faith referred to as insincerity - denying one's *self*, creating a lie (a myth), and providing oneself with an excuse for incessantly living in bad faith, for acquiescing to oppression, and becoming one's own oppressor. Beauvoir says:

> Chaque fous que la transcendance retombe en immanence il y a dégradation de l'existence en «en soi», de la liberté en facticité; cette chute est une faute morale si elle est consentie par le sujet; si elle lui est infligée, elle prend la figure d'une frustration et d'un oppression; elle est dans les deux cas un mal absolu. Tout individu qui a le souci de justifier son existence éprouve celle-ci comme un besoin indéfini de se transcender.[22]
>
> Each time that transcendence falls back into immanence there/it is a degradation of existence into "in itself," of liberty in facticity; this fall is a moral fault if it is consented to by the subject; if it is inflicted on it [the subject], it takes the form of frustration and oppression, it is in both cases an absolute evil. Every individual who has concern for justifying his/her existence experiences the latter as an indefinite need to transcend onself.

The key is to reclaim liberty and take responsibility for one's own life and choices, to continually transcend. I will turn to an explication of Beauvoir's notion of liberty in *Pour une morale de l'ambiguïté*.

LIBERTY[23] IN BEAUVOIR AND ROUSSEAU

In *Le deuxième sexe*, Beauvoir explains that

> La perspective que nous adoptons, c'est celle de la morale existntialiste. Tout sujet se pose concrètement à travers des projets comme une transcendance; il n'accomplit sa liberté que par son perpétual dépassement vers d'autres libertés; il n'y a d'autre justification de l'existences présente que son expansion vers un avenir indéfiniment ouvert.[24]
>
> The perspective that we were adopting is that of the existentialist moral. Every subject presents/asserts itself concretely as transcendence through its projects. It only achieves freedom through a continual reaching out for other freedoms. There is no other justification for its present existence except as expansion towards an indefinitely open future.

For Beauvoir, liberty in this work and in *Pour une morale de l'ambiguïté* refers to freedom from unwarranted restriction or control–institutional, interpersonal, and psychological–the right of the individual to believe and act as she chooses (or power over one's own mind and choices). As has been the case throughout this project, my primary interest in this Chapter is psychological liberty.

Although Beauvoir agrees with Jean-Paul Sartre's account of bad faith and authenticity, the unique existential ethics she puts forth is her own expansion and development of Sartre's notion of ontological liberty. In the first section of *Pour une morale de l'ambiguïté*, Beauvoir resolves problems in Sartre's attempt to work out an existentialist ethics.

Beauvoir's main thesis in *Pour une morale de l'ambiguïté* is that the fundamental principle of an existentialist ethics is liberty (on this Beauvoir agrees with Sartre). Beauvoir distinguishes between ontological liberty, social/material liberty, and moral liberty–a distinction Sartre does not make. For Sartre, there is only one kind of liberty, ontological liberty. For Beauvoir (and Sartre), ontological liberty is universal and factual, and it cannot be limited by external forces. Only one's belief that one does not possess ontological liberty can impose constraints (i.e., internal, or psychological restrictions). Moreover, for Sartre, ontologically, everyone is *equally* free. That is, the slave is as free as the master, or woman is as free as man. This is problematic for many reasons, particularly because Sartre could not explain the existence of oppression, or what motivation there is for fighting *against* oppression

This is reminiscent of Rousseau's notion of metaphysical liberty (i.e., free will). For Rousseau, women are free to live in accordance with their nature (as Rousseau and society define woman's nature), or not. According to Rousseau, women, if properly educated/socialized, will freely enter into the marital relationship and accept their subordinate status. It is in women's best interest to willingly subordinate themselves to men. Rousseau admits that women must renounce their individual liberty, but it is for their own good, the good of men, and the good of society. There is no good reason, for Rousseau, that women should fight their condition. Rousseau's education/socialization relies on females being taught, from birth, to love their duties, to want to fulfill their duties, and to believe their place in the moral order is praiseworthy and virtuous rather than a deprivation.

Beauvoir posits a second form of liberty, social/material liberty, which is in essence a combination of Rousseau's two senses of individual liberty along with his notion of civil equality in *Du contrat social* (and *pitié* can be seen in this form of liberty as well). Beauvoir's social/material liberty is also referred to as 'power,' but the sense is one of *empowerment*, or the ability to pursue projects without constraints rather than as having power over others. This type of liberty requires the adoption of *individual human liberty* as the good, or end, of human actions. This type of liberty also requires an active commitment to realizing it, or attempting to bring this liberty about for oneself and for others. Externally, this liberty refers to economic well-being and the conditions under which people live. Internally, this liberty concerns the recognition of one's ontological liberty as well as freedom from psychological constraints (i.e., beliefs that restrict one's liberty). Unlike ontological liberty, social/material liberty is not universal and can be constrained by both external and internal forces.

Beauvoir also puts forward a third type of liberty - moral liberty. As is the case with social/material liberty, moral liberty is not universal. This liberty is understood as the *choice* to recognize (or not) one's own ontological liberty and the *choice* to take responsibility for one's own life. Belief is a choice. When deeply-imbedded, previously unconscious beliefs surface, and we become aware of those beliefs, we choose whether or not to continue holding firmly to those beliefs, or abandoning them. We choose to allow others to define us and take charge of our lives, or we take responsibility for choosing our own life, we choose who and what we will become. Moral liberty also requires adopting a certain sort of relationship to other people. One must interact with others who are working to develop moral liberty, and this requires an attitude of mutual respect for the liberty of others. Moral liberty requires that others are also free—my own moral liberty depends on others being able to attain freedom from social/material constraints as well. These constraints include economic dependence, lack of opportunities in employment and life choices, and psychological dependence. Moral liberty, in Beauvoir, can only be attained in the absence of these types of limitations.

With regard to *civil* liberty, Rousseau says that "le premier de tous le biens [est] . . . la liberté" ("the first of all goods [is] . . . liberty"),[25] which "ne peut subsister sans [l'égalité]" ("cannot subsist without [equality]").[26] For Rousseau, civil liberty refers to the individual (man's) right to own property and freedom from too much government control. Civil equality refers to some degree of economic independence. Thus, we can see *some* similarity with Beauvoir in her contention that social/material constraints must be eliminated if moral liberty is to be possible. For Rousseau, this applies to men. Beauvoir extends this to everyone. This certain type of relationship with others, the element of mutual respect for the liberty of others, is evidenced in Rousseau's account of moral liberty as well—at least with regard to the social relations between men. Recall that in Chapter I, I explained that the passion or inclination of *pitié* in the civil state for Rousseau concerns the social relationships among men. This is also in part similar to Beauvoir's notion of moral liberty. Respecting one another as individual beings who possess individual liberty is a crucial element in Rousseau's project for men.

For Beauvoir, that which possesses absolute value is *choice*: the *choice* to recognize, or not, one's own ontological liberty, the *choice* to take responsibility for one's own life, the *choice* to work toward the social/material liberty of oneself and others, and the *choice* to live authentically, or not. Beauvoir says that with regard to the individual, "il y a aussi en lui la tentation de fuir liberté et de se constituter en chose .. passif, aliéne, perdu ... frustré de toute valeur"[27] ("there is also in him the temptation of fleeing/avoiding his liberty and of making himself a thing ... passive, alien, lost/wasted/ruined ... deprived of all value"). Pacifism, according to Beauvoir, is a failure to realize or pursue one's liberty. It is to relinquish responsibility (and control) of one's life to others. In surrendering power/liberty, one relinquishes all choice. This is a form of alienation, it is willfully acting as one's own oppressor, and it is *choosing* to live in bad faith. In *Du contrat social,* Rousseau says that "Renoncer à sa liberté c'est renoncer à sa qualité d'homme, aux droits de l'humanité, même à ses devoirs"[28] ("To renounce our liberty is to renounce our character as men, the rights and duties of humanity"). For Rousseau, women are *partially* human. For Beauvoir, women are *fully* human. Also, recall that Rousseau does preserve metaphysical liberty for women, he makes possible moral liberty, and preserves restricted individual external liberty, and civil liberty. This allows women to preserve their small bit of humanity. However, woman, in Rousseau, does relinquish control of her life and woman is psychologically dependent upon the opinions and judgments of others–especially men. Thus we see that possessing individual liberty (especially psychological liberty) is as important as shattering the myths about woman, and moving away from attempts to define woman.

In the next section, I will turn to Beauvoir's novelette, "*La femme rompue*" as an illustration of a woman who is *living* in bad faith (as well as reinforcing her own self-estrangement and acting as her own oppressor) to show that it is possible to overcome alienation, psychological oppression, and bad faith. Affinities with Sophie and Emma, the literary protagonists discussed in Chapter III will be evidenced, along with the traditional ideas of woman's destiny, her identity, and her purpose, as expressed in Rousseau.

BEAUVOIR'S WOMAN OF BAD FAITH: MONIQUE

Prior to writing "*La femme rompue*," Beauvoir had corresponded with women in their forties whose husbands had left them for other women. Beauvoir recognized the diversity in these women's characters and circumstances, but she also noticed significant similarities in their stories.

> Elles ne comprenaient rien à ce qui leur arrivait, les conduits de leur mari leur paraissaient contradictoires et aberrantes, leur rivale indigne de son amour; leur univers s'écroulait, elles finissaient par ne plus savoir qui elles étaient.[29]
>
> They did not understand anything that had happened to them, the conduct of their husbands appeared contradictory and aberrant, their rival unworthy of his love; their universe collapses, they ended by no longer knowing who they were.

Beauvoir says that these women were "se débattant dans l'ignorance et l'idée m'est venue de donner à voir [check original] leur nuit"[30] ("struggling in ignorance and the idea came to me to speak of their night").

Beauvoir chose for her heroine "une femme attachante mais d'une affectivité envahissante; ayant renonce une carrière personelle, elle n'avait pas su s'intéreseur à celle de mon mari. Intellectuellement très supérieur à elle, celui-ci avais depuis longtemps cessé de l'aimer"[31] ("a likeable woman but with an invasively affective nature; who having given up a personal career, she cannot take an interest in that of her husband. Intellectually very superior to her, he has long since stopped loving her"). The husband in this work, Maurice, becomes seriously involved with a female lawyer who is more alive, more open, and closer to him than his wife, Monique. "Peu à peu, il se libérait de Monique pour recommence une nouvelle vie"[32] ("Little by little, he liberates himself from Monique in order to begin a new life"). Beauvoir's objective with this work is to show, through Monique's writings in her diary, how the victim tries to escape the truth of her situation. All of Monique's efforts tend to obliterate the light, the truth, through the lies she tells herself and her lapses of memory. Every page of Monique's diary is contested through new fabrications and new omissions. "Elle tisse elle-même les ténèbres dans lesquelles elle somber au point de perdre sa image"[33] ("She herself weaves the darkness in which she sinks to the point that she loses her own image").

Beauvoir wanted the reader to approach "*La femme rompue*" like a detective novel. She sowed the seeds which make it possible to find the key to the mystery, "mais à condition qu'on despite Monique comme on despite un coupable"[34] ("but only on the condition that one tracks Monique as one tracks the guilty"). Beauvoir thought that women would look at their own situation while attempting to unlock the mystery of Monique's situation. No sentence in Monique's diary is without direction, no detail has value if not understood in the context of the diary as a whole. The truth is never acknowledged, but if one looks close enough, it is called into question[35]

Beauvoir was inundated with letters from "femmes rompues, demi rompues, ou en instance de rupture"[36] ("women broken, half broken, or in the act of being broken"). The reaction to this work was disappointing. Beauvoir says that these women identified with Monique, attributing all the virtues to this heroine (e.g., patience and understanding), and they were amazed that she would remain with a man so unworthy of her. Beauvoir says that their partiality indicated that with regard to their own husbands, their rival, and themselves, "elles partageaient l'avenegulement de Monique"[37] ("they shared Monique's blindness"). Beauvoir says that the reaction of readers to this work rested on an enormous misinterpretation. She explains: "je n'ai jamais rien écrit de plus sombre que cette histoire: toute le seconde partie n'est qu'un cri d'angoisse et l'effritement finale émiettage de l'heroïne est plus lugubre qu'une mort"[38] ("I had never written anything more somber than this story: the whole of the second part is one long cry of agony and the final crumbling of the heroine is sadder than death itself").

Others exhibited an extremely negative reaction to "*La femme rompue*," and to its author. Beauvoir says that she could not understand why this small book unchained such a degree of hatred. Beauvoir recognized that some women were disturbed by her ideas, and that they were quick to believe what was said of her by her critics. Beauvoir contends that these readers took the opportunity to make themselves appear somehow superior. One woman wrote, "Elle attend d'avoir soixante ans pour décrouvrir ce que sait n'importe quelle petite bonne femme"[39] ("She waits until she is sixty years old before discovering what is obvious to any housewife"). Beauvoir says that she was upset by the reaction of certain women who were fighting for the cause of women and who were disappointed by her story of Monique because it was not a militant work–they wrote that "Elle nous a trahies!"[40] ("She has betrayed us!").

Beauvoir says that nothing prohibits drawing a feminist conclusion from "*La femme rompue*." Monique's misfortune comes from her dependence, to which she agrees. Moreover, Beauvoir did not feel obligated to choose exemplary heroines. "Décrire l'éche, l'érreur, la mauvaise fois, ce n'est, me semble-t-il, trahir personne"[41] ("Describing failure, error, and bad faith, did not seem to me, betraying anyone"). Moreover, Beauvoir adds that in the end, the failure is overcome because even during the crisis, Monique still retains her love for the truth. She suppresses the truth, she creates myths to avoid the truth, but eventually, she can no longer run from the truth. Many readers fail to see Monique as an object lesson in failure, an illustration of how women create myths that push them into a stereotype of the abandoned wife. Some readers would rather see Monique as the blameless victim of an adulterous husband. Others reject the object lesson, pointing to the way in which Maurice and society encourage Monique to live her life through others. For example, in her diary, Monique records her preparations for a night out with Maurice. The advice from her friends can be seen as reinforcing the notion that women must use cunning and charm to get, and keep, a man.

Thus, there is the danger of breaking out of one's self-created myths only to fall into social myths.

Another way in which a feminist conclusion can be drawn from *"La femme rompue"* is that presenting Monique as a helpless victim does nothing to change the attitudes of women themselves. Beauvoir, in emphasizing acquiescence rather than harm, is addressing the elements of women's situation, which is within their own power to change. Beauvoir is always severe with the women in her literary works because she thinks it is wrong to encourage women to flee their freedom and their responsibility. The point is, women have to stop placing all the blame for the continuation of oppression on others. Women are called on to take responsibility for themselves, their condition, and bringing about change.

Finally, it is possible to read Monique's story as one of hope. Monique uses words to create her myths (she writes in her diary), and for Beauvoir, words are actions. As the story progresses, Monique begins to use words to face reality and develop a new, more independent identity. Despite her fear at the end of the novelette, Monique knows that she has to look the world, and herself, in the face, depend on herself, and *choose* her life (or not).

"La femme rompue" is told entirely from the point of view of one woman, a betrayed woman, Monique Lascombe. Monique has appropriated all of the stereotypes present in Rousseau and Flaubert. Laws have changed, but certain social attitudes have not. A dominate theme in this work is Monique's attempt to find someone to define her, to locate her identity, as opposed to taking responsibility for defining herself, for accepting her liberty.

Monique is forty-four years old, and has been married to Maurice for twenty-two years. Her story, in the form of a diary, covers roughly six months. Monique starts writing her diary after her youngest daughter has left home and before she learns that Maurice has been having an affair with Noëllie Gérard, a well-known lawyer, six years younger than Monique. The diary traces the stages by which Monique's situation gradually becomes worse–it is her *psychological* condition that deteriorates. Maurice first spends whole nights, then weekends, then holidays with Noëllie–eventually leaving Monique altogether.

Monique's diary reveals the manner in which she slips from concession to concession. She asks herself why she did not insist that Maurice choose between her and Noëllie. However, before she speaks, she concedes. Monique tells herself that, as her friends suggest, she must understand others and try to adjust herself to them. Monique writes, "En vérité je suis désarmée parce que je n'ai jamais imagine que j'avais des droits. J'attends beaucoup des gens que j'aime–trop peut-être. J'attends et meme je demande. Mais, je ne sais pas exiger"[42] ("In truth I am defenseless because I never imagined that I had any rights. I expect a lot of the people I love–too much perhaps. I even ask for it. But I do not know how to insist"). Monique describes her attempts to gain assistance from family, friends, a psychologist, a graphologist, and an advice column in the newspaper.

Beauvoir uses Monique's diary to show how she tries to escape the truth–to reveal the myths Monique has created for herself. The myths are illuminated in Monique's contradictory claims throughout the diary. She obscures the truth through omissions and new falsehoods. Clues to Monique's truth are in her account of her marriage.

It is ambiguous whether Maurice willingly gave up hospital training or if Monique more or less forced him into marriage. The question is never entirely resolved. Monique's later account of her pregnancy, which hastened the marriage, "j'ai trop faute confiance au calendrier, mais ce n'est pas de ma faute s'il m'a trahie"[43] ("I trusted in the calendar, but it is not my fault if I was betrayed") is inconsistent with her earlier claim that she and Maurice were both responsible.

It is obvious that Monique abandoned her own career as much because the realities of medicine horrified her as in the spirit of self-sacrifice to her family. The reader eventually realizes that what Monique sees as exclusion from Maurice's current research work at the clinic, where his patients do not need her, was precisely what she feared in bitterly resisting his desire for a change from his job ten years earlier. Involvement with Maurice's patients acted as a substitute for a career. It is implied that Monique is punishing Maurice for changing jobs. In reference to the former job, where she was involved with his patients, Monique writes, "je participais, je le conseillais. Ce lien entre nous, si important pour moi, il a choisi de le briser. Alors, assister de loin, passivement, à ses progress, j'avoue n'y avoir guère mis de bonne volonté"[44] ("I took part, I advised him. This bond between us, so important for me, he chose to break it. Then, to assist, passively, with his progress, I admit I did not have good will!"). This may have been a crucial moment in the marriage. Monique comes to see that, because of her refusal to acknowledge that time passes and people change, she has been living under an illusion about her relationship with Maurice for the past ten years. She has been systematically suppressing little pieces of evidence and deceiving herself into believing all was well.

Time is an important theme in this work. Monique's powers of deception are evident in relation to the present as well as to the past. Monique's initial reaction to Maurice's affair is a contradiction. First, Monique says that Noëllie is probably frigid, then she says that Maurice is attracted to Noëllie because she knows how to conduct herself in bed. Monique desperately needs this affair to be *only* sexual. Initially, the implication is that her own sex life with Maurice is perfectly satisfactory, but then she writes of his lack of warmth and affection. In spite of all the evidence, Monique continues to believe that Maurice still loves her. Here we see an example of the third type of bad faith–believing the irrational as easily as the rational, and her difficulty in dealing with Maurice's indifference.

Monique also manifests self-deception in her resolution for solving the problem. She gives in after deciding to adopt a hard line with Maurice time after time. She has emotional outbursts after she decides to be peaceful and understanding. Although she finds reasons for rejecting interpretations of her actions and her situation, as well as the advice she seeks, she continues to believe that someone other than herself, like her youngest daughter Lucienne, holds the key–Lucienne can tell Monique *who she is*–only to disregard everything in the end.

Monique's diary records the disastrous disintegration of her identity. She writes, "Il m'a suffi, je n'ai vécu que pour lui"[45] ("He was enough for me, I lived only for him"). Monique wonders if she would prefer that Maurice had died, telling herself that "la mort est seul Malheur irreparable; s'il me quittait, je guérirais. Le mort était horrible parce qu'elle était possible, la rupture supportable parce que je ne 'imaginais pas"[46] ("death is the only irrevocable misfortune; if he left me, I would survive. Death was horrible because it was possible, the rupture [between Monique and Maurice] bearable because I did not [could not] imagine it"). If Maurice had died, "je saurais de moins qui j'ai perdu et qui je suis. Je ne sais plus rien"[47] ("I would at least know who I am. I do not know anything").

Along with her self-image, Monique's perception of the past is also shattered. "Ma vie derrière moi s'est tout entière effondrée, comme dans ces tremblements de terre où le sol dévore lui-même; il s'enloutit dans votre dos au fur et à mesur que vout fuyez"[48] ("My life behind me is entirely broken, as in those earthquakes where the ground devours itself; it is absorbed in your back as you flee"). Monique realizes that there is no returning to the illusory past–everything she once believed has disappeared. Nothing survives, "pas meme la place que vous avez occupée"[49] ("not even the place which you occupied).

The end of Monique's diary is either extremely bleak, or a moment of hope. Monique writes:

> . . . je sais que je bougerai. La porte s'ouvrira lentement et je verrai ce qu'il derrière la porte. C'est l'avenir. La porte de l'avenir va s'ouvrir. Lentement. Implacable. Je suis sur le seuil. Il n'y a que cette porte et ce qui guette derrière. *J'ai peur.* Et he ne peux appeler personne que secours. *J'ai peur.*[50]
> . . . I know I will move. The door will open slowly, and I will see what is there behind the door. It is the future. The door to the future will open. Slowly. Unrelentingly. I am on the threshold. There is only this door and what is watching/lies in wait behind it. *I am afraid.* And I cannot call anyone for help. *I am afraid.*

All that is left for Monique is the present moment and the closed door of the future. Will Monique succumb to her fear? Will she transcend the past, her fear, and find her own identity, the "sentiment of her existence"? Will Monique claim her individual liberty? The end of the novelette is open-ended, and we are left wondering what Monique will choose. Unless she falls back into the habit of running from the truth, it seems plausible that she will walk through the door into the future.

NOTES

1. Nicholson, Linda. "Introduction" in *The Second Wave: A Reader in Feminist Theory*. Edited by Linda Nicholson. New York: Routledge, 1997, p. 4.
2. Alcoff, Linda. "Cultural Feminism versus Post-Structuralism: The Identity Crisis in Feminist Theory" (1988), in *The Second Wave*, p. 331
3. Ibid.
4. Ibid.
5. Ibid.
6. Ibid.
7. Ibid.
8. Ibid., p. 337.
9. Ibid., p. 338.
10. Ibid.
11. Ibid.
12. Radicalesbians. "The Woman Identified Woman" in *Second Wave*, p. 156.
13. Engels, Frederick. *The Origin of the Family, Private Property and the State*, edited, with an introduction by, Eleanor Burke Leacock. New York: International Publishers, 1985 [1972], p. 41-42, italics Engels'.
14. MacKinnon, Catherine. "Sexuality" in *Second Wave*, p. 169.
15. Wittig, Monique. "One is Not Born a Woman" in *Second Wave*, p. 266.
16. Ibid,. p. 268.
17. Beauvoir, Simone de. *Brigitte Bardot and the Lolita syndrome*. New York: Arno Press & The New York Times, 1959/1972.
18. Beauvoir, Simone de. *Le deuxième sexe I*. Paris: Gallimard, 1949, p. 29.
19. Ibid., p. 31.
20. Beauvoir, Simone de. *Le Nouvel Observateur*, quoted in *Simone de Beauvoir: A Critical Reader*, edited by Elizabeth Fallaize. New York: Routledge, 1996, p. 6.
21. Beauvoir, *Le deuxième sexe I*, pp. 18-19.
22. Ibid., p. 31.
23. Beauvoir, Simone de. *Pour une morale de l'ambiguïté*. Paris: Gallimard, 1947, pp. 47-92. My account in this Chapter is an overview of key elements in Chaptre II of Beauvoir's work.
24. Ibid.

25. Rousseau, Jean-Jacques. *Emile ou De l'éducation*. Paris: Gallimard, 1969, p. 145.
26. Rousseau, Jean-Jacques. *Du contrat social*. Paris: Flammarion, 1992, p. 76.
27. Beauvoir, *Le deuxième sexe I*, p. 21.
28. Rousseau, Jean-Jacques. *Du contrat social*. Paris: Flammarion, 1992, p. 34.
29. Beauvoir, Simone de. *Tout compte fait*. Paris: Gallimard, 1972, p. 175. © Éditions Gallimard.
30. Ibid. © Éditions Gallimard.
31. Ibid. © Éditions Gallimard.
32. Ibid. © Éditions Gallimard.
33. Ibid. © Éditions Gallimard.
34. Ibid., pp. 175-176. © Éditions Gallimard.
35. Ibid., p. 176. © Éditions Gallimard.
36. Ibid., p. 177. © Éditions Gallimard.
37. Ibid., p. 178. © Éditions Gallimard.
38. Ibid. © Éditions Gallimard.
39. Ibid., p. 179. © Éditions Gallimard.
40. Ibid. © Éditions Gallimard.
41. Ibid. © Éditions Gallimard.
42. Beauvoir, Simone de. "La femme rompue." Paris: Gallimard, 1967, p. 149. © Éditions Gallimard.
43. Ibid., p. 212. © ÉditionsGallimard.
44. Ibid., p. 192. © Éditions Gallimard.
45. Ibid., p. 133. © Éditions Gallimard.
46. Ibid., p. 193. © Éditions Gallimard.
47. Ibid. © Éditions Gallimard.
48. Ibid. © Éditions Gallimard.
49. Ibid. © Éditions Gallimard.
50. Ibid., p. 252, my italics. © Éditions Gallimard.

Conclusion

In some ways, the world of the twenty-first century appears to be a better place for women.[1] Laws and social attitudes can, and have changed since the eighteenth century. However, change is slow. Laws change quicker than social attitudes, and both are easier to change than one's own deep-seated beliefs.

For example, in the United States, women of all social and economic classes populate the work force today. According to the Institute for Women's Policy Research, "Among working women, 33.2 percent work in professional and managerial positions. About a quarter (26.0 percent) of businesses are owned by women, and 87.9 percent of women live above poverty."[2] Thus, it appears that the *degree* of the institutional oppression (or professional oppression) of women has decreased. However, as long as the wage gap exists, at least economically, women (in general) will continue to be oppressed by a system that allows women to earn less for the same work as men. In the United States, women overall "still earn only 76.2 percent of what men earn."[3] If we break this down by race, as of 1999, the earnings ratio between women and White men shows that Asian American women earn 75.0 percent of what White men earn; White women earn 70 percent; African American women earn 62.5 percent; Native American women earn 57.8 percent; and Hispanic women earn 52.5 percent of what White men earn.[4] In general, economic liberty/equality is still an ideal to strive for, not a concrete reality for women. For Sophie and Emma (the literary heroines discussed in Chapter III), there were no career opportunities. Indeed, women who were educated/socialized like Sophie and Emma were deprived of an education that would prepare them for any type of employment. The options for women like Sophie and Emma, in the eighteenth and nineteenth centuries, were to remain under the guardianship of their fathers (or another male), life in a convent, or marriage. Sophie wanted nothing other than to be a wife and mother. Emma reluctantly agreed to marriage as the best option. With Monique, women have opportunities for education and employment. It appears that Monique is not institutionally oppressed with regard to the professional realm. Monique does have the option of securing some degree of economic liberty–she can make her own money. However, it is important to bear in mind that even in Monique's time (mid-twentieth century), the wage gap was a reality. Sophie was not educated/socialized to even consider a career for herself, or to desire anything beyond her domestic role. Emma came to believe that her only avenue to liberty was through sexual relations with a man who could provide her with the material objects that came to symbolize freedom. Monique's greatest obstacles are overcoming her fear of being self-sufficient and responsible for herself, and choosing between the world (and attitudes) of the past and her present.

The institutions of marriage and the family have changed (although many in our society continue to choose the traditional marriage and family structure). It is still quite common for women and men to *say* that men should be the head of the house, that men should be the primary bread-winners, that women should be the primary care-givers, and that men should make the major decisions for the family. It appears that the dominant view in *our* society is that marriage and the "ideal" family structure consists of two parents–one male, one female. Laws and social attitudes reinforce this view. Indeed, the reluctance to pass the Equal Rights Amendment is commonly justified on the grounds that women would no longer take on their "traditional" roles as wives and mothers. Thus, at least verbally, there is evidence that the ancient beliefs and attitudes are alive and well in the twenty-first century, although not as pervasive, and women (at least in some societies) do have options.

In *American Fascists: The Christian Right and the War on America*, Chris Hedges explains the ideology of the "dominionists," or the extreme Christian right. Dominionism is steeped in radical Calvinism, and boasts such followers as Pat Robertson, Jerry Falwell, and James Dobson - religious figures with a large following–and at least one Supreme Court Justice–Antonin Scalia.[5] According to Hedges, "Dominionists now control at least six national television networks, each reaching tens of millions of homes, and virtually all of the nation's more than 2,000 religious radio stations, as well as denominations such as the Southern Baptist Convention."[6] The goal of the dominionists is to place political power and education in the hands of the radical church. Hedges adds:

> Under Christian dominion, America will be no longer a sinful and fallen nation but one in which the 10 Commandments form the basis of our legal system, creationism and 'Christian values' form the basis of our educational system, and the media and government proclaim the Good News to one and all. Labor

unions, civil-rights laws and public schools will be abolished. *Women will be removed from the workforce to stay at home* . . .⁷

It would be easy to dismiss these views as those of a few radicals. It would also be detrimental to do so. Millions of women (and men) adhere to the dominionist views. The language of the dominionists is the language used in political speeches that advocate a return to "family values." There is good reason to be concerned in our own society today, and it is important to question exactly where we are in the battle for equality and liberty. We are not so far from the eighteenth century.

Individually, females of all ages, races, socio-economic backgrounds, ethnicities, sexual orientation, etc., continue to be bombarded with explicit and implicit messages with regard to the "ideal" woman, women's sexuality, women's function, and women's place. Women continue to be sexualized, to be *for others*, to conform to the ideals of others as to what woman should be. Ali Shariati says that today, women in Western capitalist societies are "an economic product, women are bought and sold according to the value of their sexual attraction."[8] Shariati claims that "Sex has been introduced as the virtue behind contemporary art. This is why we find instant paintings, poetry, films, theater, stories, novels, etc. all concerned with sex in some form."[9] It is *women's* sexuality that is most often presented for our viewing pleasure. Shariati says that "Capitalism encourages people to consume more in order to make people more dependent upon it . . . Women are presented only as creatures who are sexy, and, other than this, nothing. In other words, woman is used as a one dimensional creature."[10] It has become commonplace to hear that "sex sells." Advertising depends on this slogan. A casual perusal through popular magazines today reveals that the selling of sexuality, making of humans a sexual object, is being extended to include both males and females. Objects, things, can be bought–and disposed of. Shariati adds that in contemporary Western society, woman "is changed into an instrument for sexuality in order to change humanity."[11] This is exactly what Rousseau does in his theoretical treatise on woman. It is up to women to make men and society better. We might be tempted to dismiss the claims of a Middle Eastern male–will it make his claims any less true? Today, as in the eighteenth century (and centuries before), women are sexually objectified. The images are internalized as "this is what it means to be a woman." As I explained in Chapter III, sexual objectification results in alienation (self-estrangement), psychological oppression, and bad faith. The sexual objectification of women, as illustrated in Rousseau and Flaubert, has not decreased, but has been extended to women in all arenas.

The greater changes *appear* to be at the institutional/professional level, but as I explained, previously, even here, change is slow. Virginia Valian maintains that *gender schemas*, "a set of implicit, or nonconscious, hyptheses about sex differences,"[12] hinders the advancement of women in the professional realm. Valian explains that gender schemas "are usually unarticulated ... unacknowledged beliefs we all–male and female alike–have about gender differences."[13] According to Valian, "Both men and women hold the same gender schemas and begin acquiring them in early childhood. Their most important consequence for professional life is that men are consistently overrated, while women are underrated."[14] Valian's interest is with regard to the professional arena. However, these gender schemas, learned in early childhood, will impact all facets of one's life and the relations between the sexes–and they begin at the psychological level. There is an intricate relationship between belief and action. Valian says that "a woman does not walk into the room with the same status as an equivalent man, because she is less likely than a man to be viewed as a serious professional."[15] The internalized gender schemas are made evident to observers through actions. Women have not progressed further in the professions because, if Valian is correct, at the deepest part of their being, women as well as men do not *believe* they are as capable and qualified as men. Insofar as my tendency is to seek out the roots of problems, it is my contention that the root cause for the slow changes for women in all facets of life are the gender schemas, the unconscious beliefs of both women and men which are based on how 'woman' (and 'man') have been, and continue to be, defined.

Can *self*-alienation, *psychological* oppression, and bad faith be overcome? Is it possible for women to live in *good* faith/authentically? Insofar as institutional, interpersonal, and psychological oppression are intertwined and mutually reinforcing, are full social and interpersonal equality and liberty possible, if psychological oppression cannot be permanently overcome? Has this chapter answered these questions? Authenticity requires constant effort, and falling back into old habits of thinking and believing, as well as acting, will remain a challenge. Moreover, living authentically requires a degree of liberty denied to women of the eighteenth and nineteenth centuries.

Of the interrelated forms of oppression, psychological oppression (my primary interest in this project) is by far the most difficult to address. Psychological oppression is the "unseen" form of oppression. If one's previously unconscious beliefs, or gender schemas, surface, a choice must be made–to remain in one's present condition, or move forward. The first step, the first movement away from psychological oppression (and alienation as well as living in bad faith) must be taken alone. After the initial movement, one will find others who have also taken that first step. External changes will affect and alter one's beliefs, but the *choice* of embracing one's liberty, of taking responsibility for one's own life, of defining oneself on one's own terms–this

Conclusion 81

is an individual choice. Seeking the assistance of others in taking the first step is to rely on others, which is renouncing one's liberty. This would be contrary to Beauvoir's understanding of liberty and what must be done if women are to possess liberty, as well as Rousseau's notion of individual liberty, and what men must do if they are to be truly free. Recall that for Beauvoir, there are three types of liberty–ontological, social/material, and moral. For Rousseau, there are four levels of liberty–metaphysical, moral, civil, and most importantly, individual liberty (external and internal). Moral liberty in both Rousseau and Beauvoir concerns a relationship of mutual respect for the autonomy of others.

Alienation, psychological oppression, and bad faith occur at all levels–the institutional, the interpersonal, and the individual (psychological). These levels are intricately linked and mutually reinforcing. My interest throughout this project has been historical, and focused on the individual level–woman's *self*-alienation, woman acting as her own oppressor, and woman's choice to live in bad faith. That is, my concern is with woman in relation to herself. I have taken the reader on an oppressive journey. Reading, or writing, about oppression to this extent can be overwhelming and leave one with a sense of hopelessness. With the application of key elements in Rousseau's concept of liberty we can find something of value for feminist theory. Thus, although Rousseau's identity politics, sexual politics, and proposed domestic education for women–as well as his overall philosophical project–do not, as I have shown, have value for feminism, we need not entirely reject Rousseau. Moreover, we can follow Beauvoir's suggestion and look to Monique as a sign of hope. If we are willing to face our demons, accept responsibility for our own lives, and *choose* to overcome, perhaps we shall. Individual liberty (understood as freedom from psychological dependence), *perfectibilité* (the ability to become other than what one is–for example, dependent, subjugated, alienated, psychologically oppressed, and living in bad faith), along with a rejection of identity politics provide the starting point.

I began this project with an internal analysis of the paradox of Rousseau's sexual politics. In addressing this paradox, contemporary feminists attempt to find something "feminist-friendly" in Rousseau's theoretical treatise on 'woman.' As I showed, within his treatise, Rousseau offers nothing of positive value to feminist theory. Moreover, as I pointed out at the beginning of this Chapter, Rousseau does share important affinities with feminism–his identity politics. I explained the implications of identity politics, from which Rousseau derives his sexual politics and justifies educating women for their role in the moral/social/political order. Identity politics, whether in the eighteenth century or today, does not provide a solution to the oppression of woman unless we simply define woman as human–and stop there. The over-emphasis on anatomical difference results in assuming intellectual difference, which leads to yet another erroneous and detrimental dichotomy–superior/inferior. There is nothing of positive value for feminist theory in Rousseau's theoretical treatise on woman, or in essentialism today.

However, as I explained in Chapter IV, we need not completely reject Rousseau. As shown, important elements of Rousseau's notions of liberty appear in the existential feminism of Simone de Beauvoir–and reiterate what Rousseau advocates for men. Recall that Rousseau does say that women *could* be educated/socialized in the same manner as men. Rousseau defines 'man' as first and foremost 'human.' Before taking his place in the moral order, Rousseau proposes that male children be taught that they possess internal individual liberty. This is the emphasis of Rousseau's proposed education for males from birth to puberty. With regard to my emphasis throughout this project (the psychological), *this* is what we can appropriate from Rousseau. All levels of oppression must be addressed simultaneously. We must give as much consideration to the forces of psychological oppression as to the other levels (institutional and interpersonal). In Rousseau and Beauvoir, psychological liberty is the catalyst for all other levels of liberty. Although Rousseau does not apply his ideas of liberty to women, he does not deny that women *could* be taught that they are psychologically independent. Overcoming oppression at all levels requires awareness, courage, action, and liberty. Women must *believe* that they are free, and they must embrace that freedom.

NOTES

1. At least this appears to be the case in our society. If we look at the global situation,
  overall, women are still denied an education, health care, and choices in many societies. As members of the group "women," what happens to individual women halfway around the world happens to *all* women. I, as an individual, have been privileged. However, my group, "women," is still greatly underprivileged–denied liberty, equality, and opportunity.
2. Institute for Women's Policy Research, 2004 Report. www.iwpr.org.
3. Ibid.
4. Ibid.
5. Hedges, Chris. *American Fascists: The Christian Right and the War on America*. New York: Free Press, 2006, pp. 10-15.
6. Ibid., p. 10.
7. Ibid., p. 12, my italics.
8. Shariati, Ali. *Shariati on Shariati and the Muslim Woman*. Translated by Laleh Bakhtiar. Chicago: ABC Group, International, 1996, p. 132. Shariati, writing in the 1970s, criticized Iranian television for failing to emphasize American women's

academic, professional, and political achievements and participation. The image of American women depicted on Iranian television was the Hollywood sex symbol and the "sexy" model. This was the image of American women Beauvoir discussed in her *Brigitte Bardot and the Lolita Syndrome*, published in France in 1959. Shariati was an advocate for women's rights–including women's right to define themselves and choose their place in society. My project is primarily historical and our society has become desensitized to the sexual objectification of women (and now, men). An awareness of how American women were presented, and perceived, by other societies serves to remind us to critically analyze our present society and to think about what we have internalized, what we, as a society, believe about women.

9. Ibid.
10. Ibid.
11. Ibid., p. 133.
12. Valian, Virginia. *Why So Slow? The Advancement of Women*. Cambridge: MIT Press, 1999, p. 2.
13. Ibid.
14. Ibid.
15. Ibid., p. 5.

Bibliography

Alcoff, Linda. "Cultural Feminism versus Post-Structuralism: The Identity Crisis in Feminist Theory" (1988), in *The Second Wave: A Reader in Feminist Theory*. Edited by Linda Nicholson. New York: Routledge, 1997.
Bartky, Sandra Lee. *Femininity and Domination: Studies in the Phenomenology of Oppression*. New York: Routledge, 1990.
Barnes, Hazel E. *Humanistic Existentialism: The Literature of Possibility*. Lincoln, NE: University of Nebraska Press, 1959.
Beauvoir, Simone de. *Le deuxène sexe, I*. Paris: Gallimard, 1949/1976.
———. *Le deuxième sexe, II*. Paris: Gallimard, 1949/1976.
———. *Pour une morale de l'ambiguïté*. Paris: Gallimard, 1947, pp. © Éditions Gallimard. 47–92.
———. *Brigitte Bardot and the Lolita syndrome*. Translated by Bernard Frechtman. New York: Arno Press & The New York Times, 1959/1972.
———. *Le Nouvel Observateur*, quoted in *Simone de Beauvoir: A Critical Reader*, edited by Elizabeth Fallaize. New York: Routledge, 1996.
———. "*La femme rompue*." Paris: Gallimard, 1967. © Éditions Gallimard.
———. *Tout compte fait*. Paris: Gallimard, 1972, p. 175. © Éditions Gallimard.
Collins Robert French Dictionary. New York: HarperCollins Publishers, 2002.
Cudd, Ann E. *Analyzing Oppression*. New York: Oxford University Press, 2006.
Dent, N. J. H. *A Rousseau Dictionary*. Cambridge: Blackwell Publishers, 1992.
Fauré, Christine. *Democracy Without Women: Feminism and the Rise of Liberal Individualism in France*. Bloomington: Indiana University Press, 1991.
Fermon, Nicole. *Domesticating Passions: Rousseau, Woman, and Nation*. Hanover: Weselyan University Press, 1997.
Flaubert, Gustave. *Madame Bovary*. Paris: Flammarion, 1986.
Gauthier, David. *Rousseau: The Sentiment of Existence*. Cambridge: Cambridge University Press, 2006.
Hedges, Chris. *American Fascists: The Christian Right and the War on America*. New York: Free Press, 2006.

Institute for Women's Policy Research, 2004 Report. www.iwpr.org.
Lee, Vera. *The Reign of Women in Eighteenth-Century France.* Cambridge: Schenkman Publishing Company, 1975.
Nicholson, Linda. "Introduction" in *The Second Wave: A Reader in Feminist Theory.* Edited by Linda Nicholson. New York: Routledge, 1997.
Okin, Susan Moller. *Women in Western Political Thought.* Princeton: Princeton University Press, 1979.
Overton, Bill. *The Novel of Female Adultery: Love and Gender in Continental European Fiction, 1830–1900.* New York: St. Martin's Press, Inc., 1996.
Pateman, Carole. *The Disorder of Women: Democracy, Feminism, and Political Thought.* Stanford: Stanford University Press, 1989.
———. *The Sexual Contract.* Stanford: Stanford University Press, 1988.
Pocket French Dictionary. New York: Langensheidt, 1992.
Rousseau, Jean-Jacques. *Émile ou De l'éducation.* Paris: Gallimard, 1969.
———. *Discours sur l'origine et les fondements de l'inégalité parmi les hommes.* Paris: Gallimard, 1969.
———. *Lettre à d'Alembert.* Paris: Garnier-Flammarion, 1967.
———. *Sur l'économie politique.* Paris: Flammarion, 1990.
———. *Les Confessions.* Paris: Gallimard, 1959
———. *Discours sur les sciences et les arts.* Paris: Gallimard, 1964.
———. *La Nouvelle Heloïse.* Paris: Garnier-Flammarion, 1967.
———. *Du contrat social.* Paris: Flammarion, 1992.
Shariati, Ali. *Shariati on Shariati and the Muslim Woman.* Translated by Laleh Bakhtiar. Chicago: ABC Group, International, 1996.
Schwartz, Joel. *The Sexual Politics of Jean-Jacques Rousseau.* Chicago: The University of Chicago Press, 1984.
Valian, Virginia. *Why So Slow? The Advancement of Women.* Cambridge: MIT Press, 1999.
Weiss, Penny A. *Gendered Community: Rousseau, Sex, and Politics.* New York: New York University Press, 1991.

www.ingramcontent.com/pod-product-compliance
Lightning Source LLC
Chambersburg PA
CBHW031555300426
44111CB00006BA/320